yes
i *am*
happy
now!

Yes I am happy now!

~ *by* ~

ARNE KLINGENBERG

Yes I am happy now!
by Arne Klingenberg

Copyright: 1999 Arne Klingenberg
All Rights reserved. This book, or parts thereof, may not be reproduced, stored or transmitted in any form or by any means (mechanical, optical, electronic and otherwise), without the prior permission of the publisher, in writing.

No permission is required for short quotations used for book reviews, articles and discussions.

International Standard Book Number: ISBN 1 876538 01 5

National Library of Australia Catalog-in-Publication entry:
Klingenberg, Arne.
Yes I am happy now!
ISBN 1 876538 01 5.
1. Happiness. 2. Ethics. 3. Self-actualization (Psychology).
4. Success - Psychological aspects. 5. Conduct of life. I. Title.

158.1

First published: January 1, 2000.

Published by:

Beam Publishing Pty. Ltd.
P.O. Box 405
Port Douglas QLD 4871
Australia
Email: editor@beampublishing.com
Web: www.beampublishing.com

Design & Cover Art by: Nexus Q, Australia.
Typeset by: K & A Collier, Australia.
Printed in the USA by Lightning Print Inc.

DEDICATED TO

Everybody

•

MY SPECIAL
APPRECIATION
BELONGS TO

Miyuki Klingenberg

Annie & Hans U. Klingenberg

Kazue & Kosaku Yamaguchi

•

Contents

Introduction:	The HQ Test	1
Chapter 1:	In The Beginning	5
	The very first step	6
	Reality check	6
	A personal experience?	7
	The Agenda	9
	Selfish by nature?	10
Chapter 2:	Choices, Choice, Choices	13
	Endless Options	14
	The smart choice	15
	Hero worship	17
	The next step	21
Chapter 3:	The Foundation	22
	Time matters	23
	No more problems	24
	No more tears	27
	Emotions vs. Feelings	28
	Escaping boredom	31
	A little trick	34
	My best friend	37
Chapter 4:	The Plan	41
	Getting started	42
	Just do it!	44
	Making it work	47
Chapter 5:	Energy Matters	52
	Some practical theory	53
	A little bit more	56
	The last frontier	60
	The mysterious Tao	62
	Rewinding the clock	66

Chapter 6:	Relationship Matters	69
	Happy communications	70
	Nothing but the truth	78
	The ultimate desire	80
	The strong	83
	And the weak	84
	Application matters	91
	Great company	96
	Your opinion, please	98
Chapter 7:	The Big Hurdle	106
	Beware, my friend	107
	False vs. real calm	109
	The grand game	116
	Past vs. present	127
Chapter 8:	Getting There	131
	The final approach	132
	Perfect health	135
	Perfect wealth	146
Chapter 9:	Love Affairs	156
	Definitions	157
	My mate	159
	Natural stuff	161
	Club members	162
	A new dawn	168
	A pleasant journey	171
	And lift-off	178
Appendix:	All Realizations	184
	Guarantee of Satisfaction	189

What's Your Happiness Quotient (HQ)? Are You Happy Now?

A Self-Test Report Card

Are you happy? How high is your Happiness Quotient? Would you like to be happier, day-in and day-out?

Yes I am Happy Now! by Arne Klingenberg is a book designed to help you find happiness in your life, regardless of your circumstances. But do you need it? Are you already happy? Here's a simple self-test that will give you a "report card" on happiness – and help you find your own HQ.

Here's how it works: Grade yourself on the following 25 statements – how close are they to the way you live your life, every day. Try not to grade yourself on your lofty goals, but on your everyday reality. This is a report card of how you approach life and happiness today – use the same standards your teachers used in school.

Be fair to yourself – not too hard, not too easy. Remember, you're quizzing yourself – so tell the truth and find out your honest answer to the question, **"Are you Happy Now?"**

Grading Scale

An "A" means you give yourself a 90%-100% grade on this question.
A "B" means you give yourself an 80%-89% grade on this question.
A "C" means you give yourself a 70%-79% grade on this question.
A "D" means you give yourself a 60%-69% grade on this question.
An "F" means you give yourself 59% or less on this question.

____ Most of the time, I have a great time!

____ I am content with my professional career.

____ I listen to my inner feelings and let them guide me.

_____ Every day, I laugh and smile a lot.

_____ I rarely become annoyed or angry.

_____ People in general, like me and my company.

_____ I don't get easily afraid or anything.

_____ I rarely feel stressed out!

_____ I adapt easily to changing circumstances.

_____ I don't feel the need to compete with anybody.

_____ My life is a great adventure and so much fun!

_____ I don't spend much time worrying.

_____ The world is beautiful and full of opportunities.

_____ I sleep very well at night and wake up refreshed.

_____ I usually focus on the solutions, and not the problems.

_____ I feel relaxed most of the time.

_____ I know my abilities and feel confident most of the time.

_____ I feel mostly fine, even when I'm alone.

_____ I have no regrets over past mistakes.

_____ To me, arguments are a waste of time!

_____ I'm always open to new ideas and concepts in my life.

_____ I live the way I choose and I let others do that, too.

_____ I don't blame or intimidate others to get what I want.

_____ If I'm not happy about something, I take the initiative to change it.

_____ I like myself the way I am.

Now, total up your grades.

Give yourself **five points** for every A: _____

Give yourself **four points** for every B: _____

Give yourself **three points** for every C: _____

Give yourself **one point** for every D: _____

Give yourself a **zero** for every F: _____

Now, Total Your Score: _____
(this is your Happiness Quotient – see below)

**For Your Report Card "Grade",
Divide Your Total Score by 25:** _____

Convert that number back to a letter grade, and you'll
have your own answer to the question, "Am I Happy Now?" _____

You've now given yourself a letter grade – just like in school – and you know if you've passed or failed. However, you can have another perspective by calculating your "Happiness Quotient." It's easy – just take your raw score and look below.

Your Happiness Quotient:

HQ of 115-125   (115-125 points)

You are a happy person, congratulations! You will find something in this book that helps you become even happier, but you don't really need it. However, since happiness is important to you, you'll probably want to read **'Yes I am happy now!'** for any insights it may offer.

HQ of 100-114   (100-114 points)

You are quite a happy person – you are doing OK. Yet, you are surely aware that you can greatly improve your happiness. So, we suggest that you read **'Yes I am happy now!'** as soon as possible. It will give you an instant boost in your daily life.

HQ of 75-99   (75-99 points)

You are a moderately happy person and can definitely improve your happiness to a large extent. Make the reading of **'Yes I am happy now!'** a priority and learn how to make happiness a greater part of your life.

HQ of 0-74   (0-74 points)

You are not a happy person – and you know it. However, there is something you can do about it and become truly happy. Start reading **'Yes I am happy now!'** right away. Take a few days off and go for it! You'll find your life is starting to change, for the better, right from the start.

If you're happy, this book will help you find new ways to remain happy; if you're not happy, this book will provide you with a practical road-map to happiness. Either way, after you've read this book and put its principles into action, we encourage you to take this test again – to see how the book is helping you to be happier, every day.

With best regards . . .

Beam Publishing

Copyright Beam Publishing – 2000 –

This quiz may be reprinted without specific permission on the following conditions:

1. That you publish the quiz unchanged and intact
2. That you credit the source as 'Yes I Am Happy Now!'
   by Arne Klingenberg,

Beam Publishing, http://www.beampublishing.com

CHAPTER 1

In The Beginning

The very first step

It may be a tough question to begin with but please honestly ask yourself the question:

'Am I a happy person?'

You know how it feels. Being joyful, playful, laughing and smiling. Totally relaxed and at ease with yourself. Feeling on the top of the world. Content. Completely satisfied.

Now ask yourself: 'How often do I feel great?' Once in a while? Sometimes? Most of the time? Can it be always?

'Don't worry - be happy!' It sounds so easy. Yet, nobody really taught us how...

How can we stop worrying when we are facing so many problems?

Reality check

How often do you see people laughing innocently, their faces made beautiful with a smile? Looking content and confident? When you walk down the street or while shopping groceries at your local supermarket? Among your friends, in your family and at work?

Try this: go for a walk in a public place when you feel really good. Your face automatically looks relaxed and happy.

You will notice how often people look at you twice, some cheering up while others look surprised, even bewildered, quietly asking themselves: "What does he/she has to laugh about in this miserable world?"!

Are we living in a happy world? How often do you hear people complaining or looking depressed – or angry?

People of all ages are visibly carrying around their sorrows. Worry wrinkles are written all over their faces, they look with stern faces into the world. Serious, even grave expressions abound. Sad and resigned looks accompany slumping shoulders and bent over postures. So many people are walking around listless, without much energy, some almost as if they wished to embrace the floor. Then there is the occasional outburst of anger and frustration.

The World Health Organization warned recently of the dangers of depression. Tens of millions of people are already affected, with many not even knowing what they are suffering from.

Is it a necessary sign of a modern and developed society? Unavoidable?

A personal experience?

What is happiness anyway, and how can we achieve it? You may say here that happiness is a personal experience and therefore individuals will have their own definitions.

That is true. One person may feel really great while fishing, another while dancing away in a trendy club.

This book is not an attempt to change your personal preferences in life. It is not concerned with telling you what to do and what not to do. There is plenty of that going on already!

And yet we can learn to be happy as we can learn anything else. Do you know somebody who is a pretty happy person? Have you noticed that their children cry less than others? Those children who are fortunate to grow up in a harmonious, caring and loving home tend to be more content and happy.

And you have probably experienced a stressed out mother in a supermarket, shouting hysterically at her crying children. Or simply ignoring them while everybody else has the dubious pleasure of hearing young people crying their hearts out.

Yes, normally, happy children grow up with happy parents. They may not always be happy, but they seem to be happier than others.

This is proof that the knowledge about being happy can be passed on. Nevertheless, we can be happy **now**, whether we grew up in harmonious circumstances or not.

As with everything else, it is nice to learn to be happy

from an early age on. It is certainly a lot easier to learn to ski when you are say three years old than fifteen or thirty years old. And if you keep practicing you will have an additional advantage again.

But it is important to realize that it is never too late...

My hope is that one day our kids can learn some methods even while at school when we as a society decide that personal happiness and self development is a curriculum worth to be taught.

There are common mistakes we all make during our lifetimes. These common mistakes will result in miserable experiences.

Do we have to be miserable? Sometimes? All the time?

Some people truly believe so. And guess what? They are often feeling miserable!

One of the first steps is to recognize what stands in the way of a happy lifestyle.

Again, we don't have to change our personal preferences at all. It is not about doing different things - it's about seeing things as they are. Realizing common-sense solutions to common mistakes and problems. How we can see and feel things differently by simply observing and understanding the basic facts of life, society at large, family life, ourselves and so on.

These are realizations which work for all of us, no matter our race, sex, religion, lifestyle, culture or circumstance.

Wouldn't it be nice if future generations could start to explore the world from a better starting point, instead of starting from the very basics the way we do? Wouldn't it be great if they didn't have to go through all the trial and errors again and again?

Being happy is not only a state of mind. It is a total experience. Happiness is not only learning to see life through rose-colored glasses while refusing to see the realities and challenges of life.

Happiness is not wishful thinking. Happiness can be real, every moment of your life. That's the goal.

The Agenda

The following chapters go through the process from A to Z, as completely as possible, based on my personal experience.

This book is not about me but about what I have been able to learn. Many things I learned the hard way. But it doesn't need to be the hard way for you.

All my life I have tried to be as happy as possible. I was always curious and wanted to know things. As a teenager I started to read philosophy of all kinds, and began experimenting with different ideas and concepts from many different parts of the world and a multitude of different cultures.

There are words of wisdom to be found anywhere if you care to look. We can progress when we are not afraid of shaking up our own belief system every now and then, questioning what we have learned and experienced.

Some philosophies led me down the wrong path, but here and there, I found precious bits of wisdom that helped me in my quest to be more happy.

Reading all these books, however, I could not find one with which I could wholeheartedly agree. I started to write down what works and what doesn't. That was the beginning of this book.

I don't like to tell other people what to do with their life and I rarely volunteer my opinions, unless I'm asked to do so. It is against my way of life and you will understand the reasons why.

But writing a book is somewhat different in the sense that only those who are really interested will buy and read it. Even discover it!

This book attempts to be a distilled description of every ingredient that real happiness consists of. A bit like a cook book.

I don't claim to have covered everything but I have surely tried.

At times, especially in the first chapters, you may find the themes discussed to be very simple, almost trivial for you, simply because you may have already fully realized those things and you know already that they are true. But please bear with me all the way and don't skip chapters. So often it is exactly what we tend to skip that we need to learn.

This book starts with the very basics and may lead you even past full graduation in the art of being happy.

You will see that what we discuss will make sense. I know because you have come this far already.

I am confident that you can truly say: **Yes *I* am happy now!** If not now, then very soon! How can I be so sure? Well, simply because it works for me! Since we are not all that different, it will also work for you. But only if you ***really want*** it to work. That part is up to you.

Selfish by nature?

Are we all egotistical beings by nature? Don't people care about others? Well, we all have to start somewhere. And normally, every person is the closest to him/herself.

That is so by default. Call it by nature or divine design, as you wish. That's how it is. Period. It is neither good nor bad.

But we soon learn that it is in our best interest to look after other people. Nobody lives alone on a remote island.

Imagine that you are stranded in a tiny life boat with say ten other people. You will quickly learn to cooperate with everybody else because it makes your life a lot easier.

Who wants to hassle and fight on a boat where there is no escape? When perhaps our own survival is on the line? Nobody will jump overboard and swim because they don't like somebody's face or behavior.

We can come to realize that the others won't simply go away, that they too are here to stay.

So for our own peace's sake, we will decide to get along. And help out each other as much as possible.

And all of a sudden we experience that it actually feels quite good to have helped someone. Of course, the person who does so and sacrifices him/herself is rare. But that is not necessary anyway.

We all affect each other someway or another. Human relationships can be too often painful. They don't need to be. And they can be also a great source of joy and pleasure. That's what we want them to be and we will look at the do's and don'ts in great detail.

Upon realizing all this we automatically start to care more and more. Everybody starts first with their closest family members and friends.

From there our caring may expand to our neighbors. Neighbors are very special and they are where they are for a reason. Just as we are. Unless we move away or they do, we are in the same boat. It is great to be able to get along. Or much better, be happy together!

Like a stone thrown in a calm lake will expand its circular waves away from the point of impact, this sense of caring may expand further and further. It can encompass people all over a particular community, country, or nation, and even the whole world.

Whether it will be a more or less pleasant journey together depends on us. And our individual strength determines how far we are willing to go.

Some will stay mentally within the narrow compounds of their immediate family or community. Some may just stay all life long at the point where we all start.

But consider this: we have about six billion neighbors...

And yet, we all start at the same point of origin – our self. And that is also where we return at the end of the day. When we take care of our most basic physical needs such as eating, sleeping and so on. We all have the need and desire for private time. This is true even for the holiest of saints or the "workaholics" of the world.

So, is the pursuit of personal happiness a selfish goal? No, because nobody can be *truly* happy at somebody else's expense.

And if you are really happy, nobody can take it away from you. I can't take away some of your happiness and think it will increase my own. Real happiness doesn't work that way. And it can not be bought or sold either.

But even from a purely selfish point of view, it is desirable to see and meet more happy people. Simply because it can increase our own happiness too! It is a lot easier to be happy among other happy people than in the midst of truly miserable folks.

Happiness is a personal experience and has no limits, so there can be no competing or fighting about it.

Also, society is made up of the total sum of all individuals like you and me. The more people learn to be happy, content and satisfied with their lives, the better off the whole world will be.

Happiness is contagious...

So, to be increasingly happy can be your greatest contribution to yourself **and** to society at large.

At this point you may already or not yet fully agree with me on this. But let's go on a journey together and explore the world of happiness!

CHAPTER 2

Choices, Choices, Choices

Endless Options

Mankind has advanced considerably in the last one hundred years and our modern lives are filled with comforts as never before. Thanks to the progress in science and technology we can enjoy an infrastructure which few of our ancestors could have even dreamt about.

Before, the struggle to provide food, shelter and doing simple things like washing dishes or clothes took a lot of time. Now these things are so much easier. We have a lot more leisure time. And we live in a world of almost endless choices.

We can choose the design and fabric of our clothes, where we live and how we live. We can choose food and drinks from around the world. We can choose what we want to learn in life, how we work and how we play; what hobbies and which sports we like; where and how we spend the next vacation.

The possible choices have become so many that we find ourselves often overwhelmed and stressed out. It can become tough to even make a choice.

Yes, I agree that not everybody has the same possibilities to choose from. It still depends on where in the world we live and how much money we have. Obviously, with increasing wealth the number of choices increases too.

But even if you are not among the super-rich, you will still find yourself blessed with a huge and often overwhelming array of choices. At times, you may wish you had more, but just think for a few moments how many you already have right now.

Look at your situation now very carefully and **write down all your possibilities**. Start with small, even trivial matters and expand gradually through all areas of your life. See all of your possible choices, regardless of whether you would actually choose them or not.

You will find that there are a lot more choices than you thought you'd have! And certainly a lot more than say your grandparents had.

The smart choice

To be happy is a choice too.
You may say that, of course, ***everybody*** wants to be happy. Is that really so? Believe it or not, but some people like to be a bit miserable. It gives them reasons to ***complain and feel sorry for themselves.*** Such people like to see and hear expressions of pity compounding their own feelings of self-pity. How come?

Others are unconsciously ***compelled to make the wrong choices*** to keep them unhappy. Even when they hear reasonable and viable alternatives to a particular situation, they prefer to choose the path which ensures them of the misery they have grown accustomed to, where changes, even for the better, sound like a risky venture.

Upon hearing a person complaining, you may offer some advice, with your best intentions in mind. But you will often find, that such advice, even if it makes perfect sense, is being rejected.

Where does such a compulsive lifestyle come from? And then there are the people who are very attracted to sad, even outright tragic TV shows, movies and novels. They sob away on their couches or in cinemas around the world.

How can you be sad and happy at the same time? Some people may like to watch, hear or read about tragedies only because it makes them feel better off. "Oh, my life is not that bad after all!"

They may derive some pleasure and comfort from such thoughts. A glimpse of relief that their life could be a lot worse than it actually is.

Are such thoughts leading onto the road to real happiness? Others again have tendencies to self-destructive and self-degrading behavior.

Does wearing a body pierce through the tongue really bring about more pleasures when enjoying some nice food?

Some people inflict all kinds of pain, voluntarily, to themselves and others. Can masochistic and sadistic practices be called signs of a healthy and happy life style?

And why do some people believe that life is not meant to be enjoyed? That they don't deserve to be happy!

Even worse, some people with this frame of mind may think that everybody else doesn't deserve it either. And do their best to spoil the party.

It is truly strange, but nevertheless so: not everybody really wants to be happy.

We will look at the reasons behind such thoughts and behavior because it will help us move further ahead on our path.

As sad as this may be, we can not choose for somebody else. Just realize how important it is that **you really want to be happy** and that you make this a conscious and determined decision.

Too many people still think that being happy is a feeling that just comes along once in while, as if by chance: **the occasional and random happy moment brought about by Lady luck.**

So they accept their frustrations and general unhappiness as just another fact of life. And never actually make the conscious decision to be happy, not to speak about following it up with concentrated thoughts and action.

The road to true happiness starts with this simple and yet powerful step. In the right direction!

R E A L I Z A T I O N   1

•

I choose to be happy!

•

Hero worship

When faced with many choices, we have to set priorities. For many people the first priority in their life is to become rich, or powerful, and if possible, famous. This age old game of competing among mankind is still quite popular. Is that really necessary in this modern day and age?

Who is the wealthiest man or woman? Who is the most powerful in the world? Who is the most beautiful person? Who is the most famous? Who is the smartest of all?

But have you ever wondered how many of our heroes are actually happy people?

We still love to read and see details about their personal lives. Magazines are full of stories about the rich, beautiful, powerful and famous. And who would not like to be included in the annual ranking of the people at the top of it all?

And yet, we can also read plenty of stories about the rich and famous becoming alcoholics, drug addicts, committing suicide, being seriously sick, going through nasty divorces, power struggles and so on. Signs of happiness? Of course not.

So, *just* being rich, powerful and famous is not the magic solution to happiness by itself.

If you are not convinced yet, go and spend a night or weekend in a really posh luxury hotel. Or at least, go there and have a drink or meal. And experience the playgrounds of the rich and famous.

For many years I travelled all over the world and, for business reasons, had to stay in the very best hotels and resorts. Tough job, I know! Anyway, what keeps on amazing me is how few of the guests seem to have a good time and enjoy themselves, even in these exquisite and very beautiful places where every of their whims is immediately taken care of! How few of the 'rich players' present actually laugh, smile and look happy. Check this out for yourself!

Some rich people live like in a mental cage where they can only eat and sleep in certain places, have to dress in certain clothes and present themselves in particular styles and manners. They have to drive certain cars and need certain status symbols. And everything, from the way they walk, talk and gesture, to even their facial expressions, is strictly predefined. You are supposed to behave like this and not like that!

Such people limit their choices along very narrow parameters and are not really free anymore. All their money and status will not buy them the mental freedom to choose and be happy.

Why is that so? Let's look at some answers a bit later on.

The competing for a place in the sun among mankind has certainly advanced our **material well-being** and increased our possibilities. It has also brought new problems like pollution and so on and we will have to increasingly deal with them. But at least the levels of freedom and comfort achieved, help us now to move on to another dimension where we can discover more about ourselves.

In the last few years many of the famous actors in Hollywood have turned to religion and all kinds of philosophies in their quest to be happier people. They realize that all that fame and money has not brought them full satisfaction, so they keep on looking for more complete answers.

Money, after all, does not buy anybody real and lasting happiness. We may buy ourselves temporary flashes or illusions of happiness, but that's about it.

You may feel happy and proud upon buying that brand new Porsche. And maybe that feeling will last for a week or two. Perhaps a little longer. But how come we can often observe people driving around in flashy and expensive cars and still wear grumpy faces?

Money doesn't buy peace of mind, it may help to avert disease but that's not sure either. It certainly doesn't stop aging and death, nor fears of death, or any other fears, anxieties and worries. And it doesn't buy *true* friendship and love.

Believe it or not, rich people often lack human warmth and affection. They are often quite lonely. The powerful and wealthy boss may be surrounded by employees of all kinds, or sales people of all sorts and calibre. What can be expected from such company?

At work they may be polite and respectful, perhaps even grateful. At worst, they may dislike their boss or be jealous. Some may be fearful of losing their job or customers and resort to false compliments. To put it nicely.

But true respect will only be forthcoming if a 'made' man or woman has earned a fortune from their own merits. Forget it, if you have received a large inheritance or won the lotto!

A rich man/woman often does not know whom to trust or confide in. 'Do they like me or are they too, just after my money?'

Who apart from paid experts will lend the troubled tycoon a sympathetic ear in times of personal crisis? Their family perhaps? But wealthy families often lack the sense of unity, cooperation and harmony found in even very poor families. There are often feuds over the family fortune and power, especially when the time has come to pass on the bucks!

This all doesn't sound too enticing, does it?

If you are rich and some of the above applies to you, don't despair. You can be happy, too. If you are not rich yet, but it is your foremost desire in life, now is the time to reconsider your priorities.

We should make our happiness to be our *first priority* in life. Not the second or third and so on, until we ultimately even forget about it.

Being happy may have been our goal in life when we were younger. But later on, when we have become so immersed in our daily struggles and in competing, we may have lost the sight of this goal. And suddenly, we have completely forgotten that all we originally really wanted out of life, is to be happy!

We can learn from the rich and famous what has not worked. Why rush in the same direction, struggle and fight with each other and be also disillusioned once we have achieved wealth, power or fame? We risk being unhappy on the way there, and especially so if we fail in our quests. We can not choose for society, but for ourselves.

Wouldn't you love to see simply happy people being portrayed in the media as new role models? Wouldn't you want to see more of how they lead their lives, and learn something about their ways, thoughts and perspectives?

When this happens, and I think it will one day, we as a society will have finally grown up.

Imagine a time when a person with a truly obscene amount of money and power, who clings desperately to what he/she has, and yet wants more and more, will not be adored any longer. Instead, people from all over the world will actually feel sorry for that person and offer some help!

Quite a happy thought, isn't it? So, let's put our first priority straight and make the right choice:

R E A L I Z A T I O N   2

•

My happiness is my first priority!

•

The next step

Hopefully, you have not misunderstood me. I love money and in a later chapter we will look at it much closer. We will give it a new meaning and see how we can have more of it!

There is absolutely nothing wrong in being rich, smart and famous, **once you are happy already!**

True happiness can and should integrate health and wealth. And we need a bit of wisdom to get there.

Just don't expect to **struggle** your way to riches, being unhappy all along the way, and then suddenly, once you are rich, you are **automatically** happy, too. It simply doesn't work that way!

But surely, it is good to have plenty of money, and combined with the proper perspective, it will also be helpful in our quest to be happy all the time.

How could we feel good when we are having aches and pains, feel often sick and are constantly worried about making enough money to pay the daily bills? It is impossible!

So, first of all, we need good health to enjoy life! And we need to have enough money to buy us all the goods and services we want to experience in our life!

But obviously, wealth should be our third priority since all the money would do us not much good unless we are fit and well. It makes sense to want it all in this order:

R E A L I Z A T I O N   3

•

I want to be happy, healthy, and wealthy!

•

CHAPTER 3

The Foundation

Time matters

We learn that we have to struggle first in life so that we can take it easy later.

This message is usually passed on from an early age in our family and later continuously reinforced by society. "You have to study and work hard in your life, or you will never make it!"

The idea to suffer now and enjoy later is again taught by various religious belief systems.

However, we also learn quite early the law of *Actio=Reactio:* every action is followed by a reaction. Every input is followed by an output.

This law goes well beyond physics: 'As you sow so shall you reap' or 'What goes around will come around'.

In Buddhism and Hinduism, this universal truth is referred to as "Karma". And the Chinese have the old Confucian saying: "If you plant soy beans, you will not harvest melons".

So, by leading an unhappy life now, we plant the seed for our future unhappiness. And the logical conclusion follows, that if we are happy now, we will also be happy in the future. After all, time is relative as Albert Einstein has shown us with his relativity theory.

Here is the problem: if we choose to postpone our happiness to a later stage in our life, we may never be able to experience it.

There are plenty of examples of hard working people suddenly dropping dead. They missed the chance to enjoy all their money!

Let us decide to be happy now, not sometimes later in the future. Get up every morning and say to yourself: **"Today is a great day to be happy!"** Never mind whether the sun is shining, or it is pouring down rain. Never mind your schedule today. Make this commitment every day, even before you get out of bed. Remember that the best time in life is now!

REALIZATION 4

•

I decide to be happy now!

•

No *more problems*

You might say now: "Hey, wait a minute! How could I possibly be happy with this lousy job? Or when I have to drive this shabby old car? Or when my boyfriend has just left me? And my boss is treating me badly? When I am terribly overweight?"

Okay. At this moment you can think of a number of problems facing you. Or a situation which you are not happy about.

And you are not alone. Everybody has some problems. And problems usually mean worries.

Even wealthy businessmen have problems to solve on a daily basis. Rich people worry about how to safely store their valuables or make the right investment decisions. Or they might worry about their health.

Is it a coincidence that business executives have the highest risk factor for getting a heart attack? After all it is their job to make tough decisions and that's where the worrying starts. "What should we do now?" or "Did I make the right decision?"

Worrying is unhealthy and certainly not a source of joy. The first step in solving the problem is to acknowledge it *calmly*. Stay in your mindset of being happy.

At the very least, remember your first priority in life. Always tackle problems while keeping the big picture in mind. Don't panic easily. Have confidence that all will turn out well.

Analyze problems as if you would not be overly concerned about them. As if *you* are not affected at all. ***Gain some distance*** and look at it from far away.

One way of achieving this is to zoom up from wherever you are at the moment. Make sure that nothing and nobody can disturb you. Then 'lift off' mentally, see yourself from above, notice your particular clothing, your immediate environment and everything else in detail. Then zoom up further and further until you are in outer space, looking down at Planet Earth.

Stay connected with yourself, but see how everything looks different now. The grand vision of things.

Or just consider your problem to be your closest friend's problem. What advice would you give your friend when you are being asked about it?

Some problems are more serious and some are less serious. Some are more urgent and some are less urgent. It is important that you make this distinction. It may not be urgent so, why get agitated about it now? You have time to let the right solution come and present itself. Very often problems go away by themselves; they tend to disappear and especially so, when you stay calm. So take it easy, relax and ***stay happy***.

Consider your options. There are ***always*** options. Some are obviously better than others. And once you know the best way, in line with the big picture, act accordingly with determination, power and precision. When it's done, trust that you have done your best and forget about it. Let it be.

If you keep on worrying whether it was the right thing to do, it will just drag you down and you lose vital energy. And another opportunity for ***being*** happy is wasted.

If you don't know the solution to the problem yet, wait and do ***nothing*** at all. Try to gain some time. Usually that is possible.

Just be still and keep on being happy. Wait until the fog clears up and the sun shines through again. Suddenly, you will know which is the best way to go. You are certain about it! Then go and do it. And again, let it be.

If you have to make a decision on the spot and you have no clue whatsoever, well, then you can always flip a coin. No, no, not to determine the decision by chance, but you might suddenly know what you want it to be while the coin is still in the air!

Sometimes, so many problems may face you at the same time and you feel overwhelmed, even outright depressed.

Take a day or two off and do your favorite activity. Go sailing. Skiing. Whatever you really like doing. Don't stay home and mull over your problems endlessly.

Try to not even think about your problems by concentrating on your hobby. **Give yourself a break and have fun. Lot's of it!**

And when you feel better, write down all problems on a sheet of paper and put it away for a little while. They are off your mind now, and on the paper away from you.

What would your favorite solution be, if you had a 'genie' in a bottle at your service?

Always take one step at the time. There is no need to rush things. One or the other problem may be suddenly gone. But so what if it's still there? No big deal!

Once a problem is solved, remember to check it off your list. Be happy about the progress you have made! This by itself can be very motivating and inspiring.

You don't have to like your problems, but don't hate them either. Consider in a quiet moment what message might be there in store for you.

'OK. I'm not particularly pleased with this situation. It is not in line with my first priority in life. Is there something I should learn about it? Hmm, I got it! Alright, so what am I going to do about it?'

Often you will find that upon learning the key message behind a problem, that it will go away easily.

Suddenly, it is gone without much further effort, smoothly and elegantly...

At the very least you will stop similar problems to keep coming up on you. Because once we have learnt what there is to learn for us, we don't need such problems any longer!

Now, let's take this thought one step further! Imagine how nice it would be, if problems don't even show up anymore in your life...

The more you have learnt the key messages of life, the less there will be the need for you to experience problems. Problems are not natural. There is *no* mean guy out there distributing them. Saying: " Oh, this person is so happy, let's throw a couple of rocks in his/her path and see whether he/she is still smiling and dancing!"

You will experience this to be a fact the further you progress on this journey...

No more tears

Whatever your problem is, don't worry about it and ***never feel sorry for yourself.***

Even if you did, it will ***change nothing***. The problem would still be there, unnecessarily taking time and energy.

The same is true with complaining. ***Never complain about anything, neither to yourself nor to others!***

It is not pleasurable to be in the company of people complaining all the time. 'Poor me' folks can be so annoying that they make some people feel like giving them more reasons to complain about!

This attitude only helps to attract predators that feed on easy prey. Becoming a victim of fraud or worse is not a happy affair and we don't need that in our life.

Remember that aggressors usually pick their victims among the weak rather than the strong. Such people are afraid of getting hurt themselves and when they feel a person's strength, even just mental strength, they will leave that person alone.

So, let's not feel sorry for ourselves and forget all complaining. This little step alone will already help us to become a lot happier!

To ask some advice or to get another opinion and discuss

possible solutions to a problem is entirely different. It is a positive and constructive move.

Most important of all is to remember, that to complain about something, acknowledges that you are not happy. You can not complain that something makes you unhappy and be happy *at the same time!*

And our first choice and priority is to be happy!

REALIZATION 5

•

I have no excuse for not being happy now!

•

Emotions vs. Feelings

What is the difference between emotions and feelings? It depends on our definition. Words need to be defined and especially so, when we discuss more complex subjects.

Let's say, you asked one hundred people to imagine a tree. Let them describe how their tree looks like. Or better still, ask them to make a drawing.

And you will end up with a hundred different descriptions. One hundred different trees altogether.

How come? Simply because it is a very individual perception. It may depend on our experiences with trees, how the first tree we saw in our life looked, etc.

This is true with all our individual ideas about what reality is like. **Reality is very much an individual experience.**

Believe it or not, but there are as many different realities on Planet Earth as there are people. Roughly six billion. Of course, we share a lot of realities. There are similarities everywhere, but if you care to take it to the extreme, we all see reality differently.

Now, in my definition, emotions are a *reactive* feeling. They are based upon a fact or an event from the past, or something anticipated in the future. For example, anger or fear. In a sense, they are not real although they certainly appear to be at times.

When we allow that our mind is taken over by our emotions, we live either in the past or in the future.

It is nice to remember some happy memory from time to time. Or when we recognize a past mistake and decide to not repeat it. We might briefly look forward to a happy and enjoyable event coming up, or imagine a dream coming true.

But we should not be going to extremes by remembering a happy part of our life over and over again. We can be happy now, too. Or live in happy dreams like watching a movie but not taking the initiative to realize them.

Our lives turn miserable when we let emotions take control over our life. Emotions, in my definition, are negative by nature. Negative in the sense that they disrupt our goal of being a happier person

Regrets. Self pity. Anger. Sadness. Worries. Anxiety. Fears. Guilt. All these are not welcome anymore. We can't be really happy when we are thrown around constantly by emotions!

As mentioned before, emotions appear to be real, but once we have learnt to deal with them, they won't be anymore. I will not suggest to just suppress these emotions, to put them in a little corner of our mind and lock them up.

No, on the contrary. We will deal with them one by one and overcome them for good!

Feelings are totally different from emotions. They are real. Feelings are positive, desirable and natural to all of us!

The feeling of happiness is an integral part of our innermost being. So is true love and friendship. Passion and

*joy. **Being relaxed, calm and confident.*** As we move along we will experience true feelings more and more. And as we do, we will be happier and happier.

So many people are not happy because they are being constantly controlled by emotions.

Living too much in the past or in the future, obviously means to not live in the present.

It is not helpful in our quest to be happier. It can be even dangerous. Let's say you are driving on the highway and your mind is all lost thinking about yesterdays' conversation with your boss. And the car in front of you brakes abruptly because a cat is running across in front of it.

Will you be able to come back to the present and stop the car before it is too late?

Living in the present means to focus our attention on every moment that is. Being alert to all that is happening around us like the Ninja warrior in the movies. We have to learn to become **mindful of every moment** in our lives and **enjoy it**.

How can we do it? It's very easy. Be aware of all your senses. Concentrate on your sense of touch, taste, smell, sight and sound. Engage as many of them as possible at each moment in time:

Enjoy the sun rays shining through the window and warming your skin. Smell the fresh and crisp air in the autumn. The laughing of children playing. Appreciate the beauty of a flower or some trees. Enjoy the tastes of every bite you eat. Admire the endlessness of the ocean. Hear the beautiful singing of birds. See the shape of the clouds drifting above. Notice the nice music playing in the background. The looks of a beautiful person.

Whatever it may be that you find enjoyable. Take the time to notice it. And just enjoy it! Anybody can do it and it doesn't need to cost a lot of money either. You know the saying: "The best things in life are free." They truly are!

Joking and laughing is free. Exchanging love is free. The beauty of nature is free. True friendship is free. Feeling great is free, too....

It may be only small things at a time that you find pleasurable. But enjoy them nevertheless.

Every time that you are too busy to notice, absorbed in the past or the future, you will miss them.

And as we become more mindful of every moment, we will automatically avoid silly misfortunes like, hitting the head when rushing out of the car, banging the knee on a desk, and the like. More often than not, such incidents and even bigger accidents are a result of being mindless and can be avoided.

It is always now. And always enjoyable so!

REALIZATION 6 ~ 7

•

I can enjoy every moment of my life!

•

I am mindful all the time!

•

Escaping boredom

What makes our life boring and dull? Most people experience this at some stage in their life.

Normally this happens when we get older and we feel that we know it all now. We have experienced what there is to experience. Or we think that some experiences are simply beyond us. Maybe for monetary reasons, maybe because something sounds too risky and dangerous. Or we may have to sacrifice a little bit of physical comfort...

Well, there is something else. It is called daily routine. When we do the same things every day, over and over again.

We wake up and go the bathroom. Take a shower and get dressed. Eat our corn flakes or whatever. Go to work. Work. Have lunch. Work some more. And so on. You get the picture.

Life then becomes **automatic**. Nobody adds something new and exciting. It has become all the same, like chewing over the same food a hundred times.

To live a life switched to automatic mode is rarely a very enjoyable affair. It may give us a false sense of security and purpose in life. Most often it just happens over the years. Routine and habits become so ingrained until we don't notice it anymore. It has just suddenly become a fact. Booorring....

We drive the same route to work every day and because all the sights are so familiar, we get lost in our thoughts and especially, here it comes again, our emotions.

It is very important to step out of our routine behavior. Let's make a conscious, mindful decision every moment of our lives...

Let *us* add new spices into our life. Because if we don't do it, nobody else will either!

In the beginning it may take some effort to break free but we will quickly realize that it is a very rewarding experience. To allow new things to happen. To meet new people. Do things we have never done before. Seek out all the pleasures the world has to offer to the adventurous...

So let's sometimes take a different route in the car and explore new roads. Do things at different times than normal. Try new tastes of food and drinks. New styles of clothes. Travel to new countries for holidays.

Remember how exciting the world looked like as a teenager? How about doing some crazy things?

Drive to a lonely beach at night with your partner and/or some close friends. Bring a table and chairs, with white linen, your nice cutlery, the whole lot. Have a five-star course under the stars, with the waves gently rolling in. The girls dressed in holiday beachware, the boys in bathers and tuxedo shirts. Some champagne perhaps? And stay put when the tide rolls in until say, your knees get wet...

To live a more spontaneous and fulfilling life is a lot easier when we plan less in our lives. Let things happen and take notice what is happening around you. Then when you feel like organizing, joining and having fun, just go for it! Have fun and enjoy it!

The best parties always just happen, they kind of fall out of the sky. So let's not tie up ourselves in tight schedules all the time, unnecessarily.

Some people love doing just that. They follow terribly busy timetables throughout their lives. Maybe because it gives them the feeling of being needed, or they feel more important and secure. And afterwards they complain how busy they are and how little time they have for themselves. I call it 'homemade' stress...

Have you ever met an old school friend that you haven't seen for many years and all you can say is: "Hi, how are you?" And you had no time to really listen to the answer, already rushing on for that next meeting? Later, you may have thought: " How nice it could have been to go for a drink together and chat for while!".

During my business years I flew at least three times a year around the globe, visiting many places. Each trip took me about two months. I was always stressed out and followed a very tight schedule. My whole life was organized like a Swiss train schedule.

And I used to get terribly upset when things didn't work out as planned and scheduled. After many years of causing myself and others considerable pain in trying to stick stubbornly to the plan, I got sick. And I had to take it easy. I was forced to let things flow in their natural order.

Suddenly I noticed that strange things happen because I let them happen. My business approach became very flexible and I followed the energy of the situation. I may have planned a trip to Hong Kong, but suddenly found myself waking up in a hotel in Rio de Janeiro.

It took me a while to get adjusted to my new life. **Going with the flow.** But business has improved tremendously. And as I became more at ease with myself and enjoyed each moment, my smiles got broader and broader again.

Surprise yourself and others with your flexibility, your freedom of mind to change!

There is no need to be afraid of changes. Discover the magic of changes. Of course, always to the better!

REALIZATION 8 ~ 9

•

I don't mind changes!

•

I am very flexible!

•

A little trick

Remember, I just mentioned my smiles were getting broader again. That's right! This is definitely a good trick to remember.

One easy way to enjoy the moment is to laugh a lot. **Happy people find always something to enjoy and smile. Something to joke about and laugh.**

It is so natural. Have fun here and now! Even when

things go wrong we can find a reason to laugh. Because in every situation, no matter how serious it looks at first, there is something comic or funny.

With a good sense of humor, life becomes so much easier and enjoyable. If you can really see nothing funny in a situation and you feel depressed or sad, go and see a funny movie. Or listen to a tape with jokes. And suddenly the ice breaks and you are in a good mood again. Laughing is not only great medicine for the soul, but it relaxes our body too.

And when we are relaxed, everything else will progress a lot smoother. Another way which works great is to go in front of a mirror and make funny faces to yourself. You may be in a tough meeting where everybody is so tense. Excuse yourself for a moment and go to the bathroom.

And then go for it! It may be tough in the beginning and you may not think it's funny at all. But keep going anyway and soon you can laugh even at your sour, sad, worried or sorry-looking face.

Try to make all kinds of grimaces, as many as you can and you will be surprised of what you are capable of. Then back in the meeting, you may crack a joke and lighten up the atmosphere. If that's not appropriate, well, just continue to have fun by yourself. Quietly within.

Chances are good that whatever you wish it to be, the outcome of the meeting will be to your satisfaction!

Seriousness is definitely a disease. And a lot of people seem to be affected by it. Just look around. Or switch on the nightly news. Stern and serious looking people taking themselves, their position and problems soooooo seriously. It is sometimes extremely funny to see!

Kids learn this disease from adults. So, let's learn from our kids to become playful again. Cheerful, joyful. Pure and innocent.

You know the difference between childlike and childish... Even if we have an important position to play in society, we can do that in a lighthearted way.

Nobody is so important that he/she can not be replaced by somebody else. This is even true for the president of a country, no matter how that person would disagree, it is still a fact.

It is important to take ourselves serious in the sense of a healthy level of self esteem. But, please not too much, or else it becomes funny! And remember that if you can not laugh about yourself, somebody else will...

Of course when we crack jokes and laugh, we should never do it maliciously and with bad intent in mind. Don't laugh at people and feel better than them. It is entirely different to laugh at a comic situation or a funny mistake made, than it is to laugh about somebody in a mean or personally offensive way.

That cannot keep us happy and we will discuss the reasons why a bit later. ***Make it a habit to walk through life with a smile.*** Even pulling up the angles of the mouth just a little bit in an almost unnoticeable smile will help us to be more cheerful and take things easier. It actually releases positive chemicals in the brain and relaxes the body. And you probably know that we need a lot less muscle activity in the face when smiling compared to making sour and serious looking faces.

So let's save that energy for being happy instead! And by the way, a smiling face looks a lot more beautiful, too...

The Chinese use the technique of the 'Inner Smile' consciously for centuries and go even further by sending that smile all over the body, even into specific organs.

Give it a try, it works! It is great when we can look at life with a smile and find that it is not such a serious affair.

And our problems especially so.

REALIZATION 10~11

•

I love to laugh and smile!

•

I can see funny things all the time!

•

My best friend

So now we know how to the enjoy the eternal present. Of course, as with everything, continued practice will make great masters...

But have you noticed something? It not only helped us to already being happier but something else is happening.

By living now, we allow our internal guiding system to express itself! You may call it your instincts, your intuition, your hunches, the inner voice. Whatever.

For the remainder of this book, I chose to call it 'my best friend' because it has only my best interests at heart. The word intuition explains itself: 'in'- inside, internal, and 'tuition'- teaching.

We all experience intuitive moments in our lives. Some people more than others because they follow this ability more often. It is not because they are smarter, wiser or more advanced, whatever that is supposed to mean. Let's put the record straight here:

Intuition doesn't need to be learned or earned. We all have it. It is an integral part of our being. It is one of the true feelings!

The only time we can not access it is when our mind is too cluttered up with emotions... When all kinds of negative and destructive thoughts race uncontrolled through the mind. Clear distinction becomes very difficult and we can easily dismiss the valuable input as just another voice among all the other noise.

Intuition originates from different parts of our mind of which we are usually less conscious. We may call it the sub-consciousness. And there is a link to our innermost being. But more about that later.

Even if we don't know exactly about its origins or how it works, we can still benefit greatly.

It doesn't mean that the messages we receive are less important than our rational or analytical thinking. Just remember that most vital body functions, from digestion to blood pressure, from the immune system to the heart valves and so on, are all controlled by a nervous-system switched on auto-pilot. Luckily, our opinion or approval is not required.

Intuition works a bit like an auto-pilot system, too. All we really need to do, is be still and listen within.

And take the time to notice the messages we receive. By being in the present!

The system works non-stop whether we like it or not. Whether we notice it or not. Regardless of our opinions. It is just there for our benefit.

Suddenly a message is flashing through the mind.

It may be a strong feeling. An impulse. An urge. A flashing word. A picture. A vision.

Sometimes, when we are looking for an answer to a question we can randomly open a book and read the first sentence. All of a sudden we know what we should do. A keyword provided the solution.

Or during a conversation, even with a stranger, we hear some kind of a story. And suddenly it clicks and we can see the answer we were looking for.

You may have experienced something like going in a shop out of an impulse without a real need to buy something. You just followed 'a hunch'. And there you may bump into an old friend you haven't seen for ages. You can be sure that something pleasant will arise from this meeting by 'chance'!

Or we feel angry about somebody. Suddenly we meet that person in the elevator of a public garage. Where there is no escape and we cannot pretend we haven't noticed. Wrong time in the wrong place?

Nope. Because now we have the chance to clear the air. And we can end up making peace again.

It always tells us something. There is always a reason, whether we can recognize it at the moment, or not. It is not important to know the reasons.

The results of following our true feeling or intuition is always positive. It may not look like that at first sight, but looking back in time we know this to be true.

Any aspect of our lives can improve a great deal when we choose to listen. In our private, professional and social life.

Even our investment decisions. How many successful investments did you make by following the advice of your newspaper editor, your broker or friends?

Probably not too many. I didn't. It worked better for me when I followed my feelings. And as a trained economist with some market knowledge I'm supposed to know these things. Right?

Well, not really! Of course some knowledge can be helpful. But that may not help much to predict the future course of events. And that's what investment decisions are all about!

We can over-analyze a situation and become just more confused. Professional analysts with access to an abundance of information get it very often wrong. Because even when we are correct with our prognosis, we have to get the timing right...

Often when I had a strong feeling and ignored it, things turned out the wrong way. I could fully understand later on that I had the right answer all along. And could have saved myself a lot of upheaval...

To get the message is only half of the process. We have to trust it wholeheartedly and follow it up with some action. Or sometimes non-action – stopping everything and being still.

A good time to learn being in tune is while in bed, before falling asleep and right after waking up. Don't rush out of bed in the morning. Take your time and enjoy these reflective moments to the fullest!

To follow our intuition means to do the right thing at the right time. Let's choose to listen and follow. More often. Always.

REALIZATION 12 ~ 13

•

I listen to my feelings within!

•

I trust and follow my feelings!

•

CHAPTER 4

The Plan

Getting started

Now we need to make some more choices and I suggest that you make yet another list.

Find a quiet moment and place and take your time to do it carefully. Make sure that your mobile phone or beeper is switched off.

It is very important that you are quiet within, in tune with yourself. Write down everything that you really like. Small things, big things, everything that you find enjoyable and pleasurable. What you like doing and what feels good to you.

It doesn't matter if something is out of your reach at the moment. Dreams which may look fancy now. Never mind, just write it down anyway.

After that, write down all the things that you don't like doing. And anything that feels bad to you.

So now you have it all on paper. A plus column and a minus column. Great, we are getting there!

Here let me add a few words of caution. Be very sure that everything you have written down are really your dreams or nightmares and not somebody else's.

Too often our choices become influenced by projections of our parents, other close family members or friends. It is quite normal that parents have big dreams and expectations for their offspring. They want their kids to have a better life and often deny them the right to choose independently.

It is one thing to make sure children get a great education. But, to choose a subject for them which they may not like or not be suitable for just to improve their chances for a better income, is quite another. Different economies have different requirements at different times. But to choose study subjects just with money concerns in mind is definitely the wrong way to go.

Sometimes, parents in the course of their lifetime 'forget' to realize the dreams they had when they were kids. And now want their children to do it for them. Sounds familiar?

In some places where society is very restricted for cultural, political or religious reasons, the peer pressure to do certain things or not to do certain things becomes enormous.

If some of the above applies to you, don't harbor any resentments for the past. Have confidence that the intentions were always good. ***But know that we are here to realize our dreams and not to fulfill other people's expectations in us... So make sure that you now choose for yourself!***

Be aware that you are now making the most important choices of your life and that it will affect the rest of your life. And you want it to be a very happy life! Right? And ***This*** is it!

OK. Now, imagine that money is no concern at all because you have fifty million dollars in your bank account.

YES! Fifty million dollars! It is all yours to keep and you can choose to do anything you like!

What do you want to do now? What do you choose? Write it all down again.

And remember that just doing nothing, getting fed by your chef and served by your butler or maid, may not be a long term option. You may have had dreams of just going to the beach and doing nothing at all. Absolutely nothing.

That's fine! It is a very nice experience. And you may enjoy it for a month, maybe six months or one year. Or two years. I have done it and believe me, after a while it will get boring. I still love to go to the beach, but not every day!

We need to be active and do something with our lives. Give ourselves a direction and some purpose. There is a reason for each one of us to be here. We all have our unique gifts and abilities. There are some things that we really like to do and we are just good at it! Simply because we love it.

If you don't know the answers yet, then maybe you should really go to the beach for a while! Or the mountains or wherever. Away from it all. The place where you spent most of your time – home. Go away and find a beautiful place. It doesn't need to be very far away although that can help too. It doesn't need to be for very long either. It may be just for a couple of days or a weekend.

"I have plenty of money. What do I enjoy? What do I want to experience?" Reflect on these questions deeply from within.

Now let's compare what you wrote down before and after you had the fifty million dollars.

Are your dreams and your favorite activities still the same? They should be with the only difference that there may be more selections after you had the fifty million dollars. Because now you have more possibilities to choose from.

R E A L I Z A T I O N   1 4

•

I know what I want to experience and enjoy!

•

Just do it!

OK. Let's come back to the present. You may not have the fifty million dollars right now. But why should you not have it if you really desire it? Or whatever else you desire? Dreams can become true.

We need to have the confidence that they can become true. It will be a lot easier and we will discuss this a lot more.

Remember that most of the really successful people have reached their goals because they enjoyed doing what they did. They made their preferred activity, their hobby if you will, into their profession. And they don't even feel that they are working...

When you love doing something, it is obviously enjoyable and you are good at it. And you will get better all the time because you want to get better.

For example, if you love surfing, you will always do your best to improve it. Not on somebody's orders but because you want it. Anything that we do in this way will become also very successful... You will certainly not count the time anymore as you may do in a boring and unfulfilling job.

"Oh, it's only two o'clock. Phew, another three hours to go!" No. Instead you too will be able to say: "Gosh, I can't believe it's already eight o'clock!"

Time seems to just fly by when we do something we truly love. *Know what you like and do these things more often.* You may not be able to do them all the time yet, but if you really want to, and make some efforts to get there, you will.

Know what you don't like and do these things less and less often. It may be a gradual process, step by step, until you finally don't do these things anymore. Because you don't need to. And because you don't want to.

Let's say you made the wrong choice and have a job which you are not happy about. Maybe you had not many choices at all. So think of how you can get out of this situation. Don't just quit right away as you will still have to pay the bills. But prepare yourself for the time when you can quit.

Expand your horizons. Learn new things that you like and will help you along your way to realize your dreams. It is never too late to learn more...

I know that in some countries it may not be the fashionable thing to do, nevertheless, it is a recipe for success and happiness:

Live according to your present means. To borrow to sustain a fancy lifestyle you can't afford yet only opens the door for worries and a big bang further down the road!

Save as much of your income as you can. Do your

favorite things as often as possible and think of how you can make money doing them. Then go for it in your spare time and suddenly you have arrived.

You can now quit your job and do the things you really enjoy! But even when you have to do something which you don't like, be happy anyway. Enjoy yourself .

Be conscious of what you do, take pride and pleasure to do it right. Try to constantly improve your performance. It can be your nice little private challenge and you never know, somebody may notice it too, and you might get a pay rise. And the quicker you will get out of there.

You know the old saying that if a job is worth doing, it is worth doing it well...

The more we apply this to anything that we do, see clearly the reason why we do it, and then doing it thoughtfully, mindful of every moment, the more we increase our happiness.

Most people spend most of their time on their jobs, besides sleeping perhaps, so it is great when we can be happy there, too, instead of feeling sorry for ourselves and spending the days swearing and sweating in a grumpy mood.

Believe me, I had some pretty awful jobs doing very dirty things which nobody else wanted to do. Jobs where you would love to have a job as a dishwasher. But I made money doing it and it helped me to move on. I just decided then that I might as well be happy doing it, not just before or after the job!

The physically hard and dirty jobs I had I decided to consider as 'exercising'. Every move I tried to do carefully. I enjoyed the progress I made in controlling my body. And the feeling of becoming better and stronger all the time. And I didn't need to spend money going to the gym after hours. I got paid for getting fit and I had more leisure time than some of my buddies!

Always remember the big picture. Your Plan. Your priorities in life. Know the reason why you are doing what you have to do now. And know that is just a temporary situation along your path. Soon you will only be doing what you enjoy the most!

You know, the word "careful" is made up of two words – care full. Full of care. ***When we care enough for our life and therefore everything that we do, then everything becomes important and worth enjoying, even going to the bathroom or brushing teeth.***

The more we care the happier our life becomes. It is important to appreciate every moment, every activity, no matter what. And see things in a positive light all the time.

REALIZATION 15 ~ 16

•

I can always see something positive!

•

I am careful and enjoy myself all the time!

•

Making it work

Does life have to be a struggle? How can I achieve my goals without too much effort?

These are legitimate questions and not just for lazy people. I have always been lazy in the sense that I like to get what I want without any unnecessary sweating. That is not exactly what we were taught in school or by our parents. But there is nothing wrong in taking a short cut as long as we get where we want to get.

You know, life is a bit like travelling on a road. Let's say that cars are our bodies, and our minds are driving them. Some drivers like to drive automatic cars because it's easier and requires less effort. Maybe, they don't make many decisions in their lives and let others decide for them.

Others prefer a manual transmission because it gives them better control. Maybe they know what they want out of life and are going for it. And yes, there are those that drive an automatic and know what they want, too, but like to make the trip as enjoyable as possible at the same time.

Some people drive big cars and some small ones. They come in all kinds of colors. There are cars that are well-maintained and looked after while others are moving rustbuckets!

Some drivers just cruise slowly and are not in a hurry at all. They don't mind being stuck in slow traffic and taking things as they come along. Others are constantly rushing through the city and countryside without much care of the outside world.

There are people who know where they are heading or which roads to take. Others are not sure and just wonder around hoping to find their destination sometimes.

When lost, some immediately ask for directions or consult their map. And others refuse to do that because they think they know it best anyway.

Then there are the road bullies who like to cut you off just for a bit of a thrill. Aggressive drivers may think that it is their right to be ahead of you and don't care to endanger others in the process. Others are considerate and safe drivers. Some are drunk or almost falling asleep, and wonder why they suddenly wake up at the bottom of the canyon. Or maybe they don't wake up anymore.

Some get easily agitated, while others keep their cool. Some are whistling and singing along the way while others shout, scream and push their way through life. If you like, you can take this further and further, as far as you want to. You know now where you are heading and you want to be happy along the way. Right? *So let's take the easy and quick way and not the long and bumpy one. That's the smart way. And it's the happy way, too!*

Our mind can be trained to do just that. Let's see how it works and talk some more about cars. Sorry, girls!

Say, you are considering buying a car and finally you have chosen a Toyota Camry, or whatever else you like. This is the car you really want, in the price class that you can afford. Now drive through the streets, still in your old car or, in the new car, if you bought it already.

Suddenly you seem to notice every Toyota Camry on the streets; whether they are parked, driving behind or in front of you, or coming in the opposite direction. You see this car more often than any other car and you may wonder and say: "Wow! This is quite a popular car!"

But when you changed your mind before purchasing the Toyota, and you fixed your mind on another car, you now notice this car all the time. And you didn't before!

It doesn't matter which car you choose, and it is not limited to just one car, or the ones you can afford to buy now. It may be the Mercedes Roadster you are dreaming about, and seeing all the time.

Or try this: take this or any other book, magazine or newspaper. Concentrate your mind on one word for a few moments. The eyes are closed and you picture this word clearly in your mind. Spell it out mentally.

Now open your eyes and look directly at the open page without looking at something else first. And you will see that the word on your mind seems to almost jump out of the page, every time that word appears!

Our mind works a bit like a search program in a computer. When we focus our attention onto something, it will be registered in our mind. And then our mind is constantly observing and searching all the information coming in through our senses for the preferred input.

It filters everything through, remembers what we want to

notice. Automatically, we will notice these things more often. Or it filters out the less preferable choices. More precisely, the information is put in the proper perspective with a lower priority of awareness.

Imagine happy people in your mind and focus on this picture for a while. And you will see, even meet, more people that are smiling and laughing. Catch the happy moments of others and enjoy them, too. ***Appreciate happiness in all forms and shapes.*** Be happy to see others being happy. And being able to be in the company of happy people.

You will still notice others with sour or mad faces, but you will not look at them for long. Because that is not a particularly beautiful sight and you simply don't enjoy it.

We can program our minds in any way we want and we can do it consciously. It is like installing new software or reprogramming the old one.

What we want to see we will see more often. When we have made up our mind on something, we will get more and more evidence to support this view. And notice less and less the evidence which contradicts this present viewpoint. The stronger we concentrate on an issue the quicker we will see the results of this process.

You will surely appreciate now the time and effort you have made in clearly knowing what you want. It is veeeeeeeerry important.

Just imagine for a split second what happens to a person who hasn't made all these conscious decisions and choices. And concentrates all day long on problems and all the past, present and probable future miseries experienced, respectively to be experienced. Phew. Thanks, but no thanks!

You can easily experience this: ***focus your mind on beauty and you will see increasingly more beautiful things in your life. And when we decide to enjoy our life and concentrate on all that we enjoy, we will experience more joyful moments all the time.***

So ***now*** focus strongly on your Plan, with all your happy choices and decisions, and they will become reality. More and more all the time!

You may not be fully convinced yet, but that's how it works. So, just do it anyway. And as we move further along together, you will see and agree...

Take up your list again and again over the coming days and weeks. Anytime you have a quiet moment for yourself. Concentrate on every of your desires, wishes and dreams.

All that you want to experience and all that you enjoy.

R E A L I Z A T I O N   1 7

•

All my dreams can become true!

•

CHAPTER 5

Energy Matters

Some practical theory

Let us make a bit of an excursion here before we move on and look at what this all means for us.

The first question is: Matter and Energy. What is the difference?

There used to be quite a gap in the understanding between East and West, between modern science and the ancient knowledge of Asian cultures.

As our knowledge of the world and its workings increases, we can see that there are no more differences in both viewpoints. That they actually complement each other.

Modern science has improved tremendously in the last fifty years and still continues at lightning speed. Many of the old theories and conclusions have long been abandoned and been replaced with a more thorough understanding. Study books become obsolete or in need of frequent revision.

Now we know that atoms, which were once thought to be the smallest particles of matter, are made up of tiny electrons, protons and neutrons. And as the search for finding the smallest of all particles continues, always tinier and more exotic particles have already been discovered. Here is a selection: leptons, electron, muon, and tauon neutrinos, pion, kaon, K and eta mesons, proton, neutron, lambda sigma, xi and omega baryons.

Some particles making up matter are just flashes of energy, or put differently, light.

Just very recently, it was discovered that neutrinos have mass, approximately one ten-millionth the mass of a tiny electron, contrary to all the previous beliefs 'written in stone'.

This discovery now forces scientists to rethink the shaken up "Standard Model", a theory of subatomic particles based on the research of the last 75 years!

Thanks to all the progress made in quantum physics and ever-improved electron microscopes, we know now, that matter is not as solid as it appears. ***Everything has become*** *relative; a matter of perspective rather than a necessary cause of arguments. We can choose whether we see a rock as solid matter or as mainly empty space where super-tiny particles of energy rotate at lightning speeds. Both viewpoints are correct.*

To clearly understand that all there is – the world, our bodies and all matter – can be expressed as moving energy, opens the door to further and deeper knowledge. The knowledge of who we are and how mind and body are connected. How disease can be cured more effectively. How we can live comfortably on Planet Earth without destroying it and depleting its natural resources. And improving the ways we interact with each other, eliminating suffering as much as possible and increasing our happiness.

All the energy particles making up the atoms oscillate at different speeds per time unit, or frequencies. A low frequency indicates less revolutions per second, and a high frequency, more.

We know that lower life forms like bacteria or viruses vibrate in the ultra low frequency range. Household appliances are powered in the low frequency range of around fifty to sixty hertz. Sound waves are rotating in higher frequency ranges and can be measured beyond the range our ears can perceive. Slower rotating sound waves can induce feelings of fear even though we do not hear them. If you have a dog, you know that you can send commands with a special whistle, where the sound waves vibrate at a level too high for us, but not the dogs.

Light again is vibrating at much higher speeds than sound. The visible light range for us humans ends with the infrared light on the 'slow speed' side of the range and the ultraviolet light on the 'high speed' side of the range. But bats can see and navigate at night because their bodies are built to perceive the high velocity x-rays. Birds are shown to have UV-vision in recent research, besides having our 'normal' vision. And astronomers measure gamma rays with special telescopes to learn more about distant stars and galaxies.

So, as the instruments of measuring frequencies get better all the time, the known frequency diagram is expanding, too.

There is always an underlying reason for energy to flow. It never happens out of a coincidence. With electricity it is quite easy to understand why the electrons flow. Elsewhere, it may be more difficult to explain the reasons why energy flows or something happens. But even if we don't know some reason yet, it is never happening just by chance. We use the words "chaos-theory" or "coincidence" whenever something can not be explained.

Remember that every action brings a reaction. Maybe we can at times just witness an effect and not understand what caused it yet. But there is always a cause.

And thanks to Albert Einstein we know that *energy can never just disappear or be destroyed, but rather changes its form or appearance.*

We cannot make water disappear no matter how hard we try. We can separate the hydrogen molecules from the oxygen or change its form from liquid to solid or gas. But we can not make it disappear. And sooner or later those same atoms will again become water.

The micro-cosmos and macro-cosmos are identical except for their size. Or put differently, ***the inside and outside world are mirroring each other.*** In the universe and within the atoms making up our bodies, tiny respectively huge particles whirl through mainly empty space. Normally, they move within their assigned orbits in the proper velocity.

When everything is right, there is harmony. The word cosmos is derived from "cosmo", the Greek word for order.

And if something is out of balance it will result in a temporary disharmony or disorder. Eventually the balance is always restored, one way or another.

So now we understand these principles and know that they are universally valid. Let's review them briefly.

REALIZATION 18~21

•

Everything is energy rotating at different vibrations!

•

Every cause produces an effect, every effect has a cause!

•

Energy changes its form, but continues to exist!

•

What is within, is without.
The external reflects the internal!

•

A little bit more

Hopefully you will not think you were thrown back in time to your physics class. You may not find such discussions very interesting and yet, the practical applications will be very helpful in our quest. So, please be patient with me!

Here is another universal principle to all flows of energy: All particles that oscillate, whether on a micro-or macroscopic level, create in the process an energy field.

Depending on our viewpoint, we may call it an electromagnetic field or gravity. And when we discuss our body and its subtle aspects, it is called bio-field or aura.

The traditional methods of healing in Asian cultures, from India to China and Japan are being increasingly used and integrated with western medicine. The understanding of the eastern systems is based on the knowledge of the flows of energy in our bodies. In India this energy is generally referred to as 'Prana', in Chinese 'Chi' and in Japanese 'Ki'. They make a distinction between various forms, depending on its function and vibration level.

Western researchers measured this subtle energy, bio-force or ether, in humans, animals and plants and photographed the corresponding fields of energy, the biofields, with special equipment and cameras.

This electro-photography was discovered by Nikola Tesla, Michael Faraday and Thomas Edison almost a century ago. It has been further researched by Semyon D. Kirlian in the 1930's and has become more widely known as Kirlian photography. They concluded that the biofield contains all the basic information for the organization and building of cells. *Harmony in the energy fields always resulted in a healthy condition, while dis-harmonious patterns were observed when a disease was present.* So, the bio-force or ethereal energy has an important influence on our body functions and well-being.

In China for example, it is common knowledge that *our emotions have a strong effect on our energy levels and its balance.* They say that we lose this energy, chi, whenever we feel angry or sad, are worried, depressed or fearful. And it makes sense when you remember how exhausted you felt after a day of worrying, or after a big shouting match.

In the next chapters, we will discuss emotions more in detail and see how we can eliminate all negative effects and save energy for something better – doing what we enjoy the most and being happy!

Low levels of Chi makes us feel bad and severe inbalances causes us to become sick. And whenever we have plenty of this energy, we usually feel great and everything is ok.

We can influence our energy level positively by eating in a balanced way. Natural foods are more powerful than highly processed foodstuff. But even processed foods will regain higher energy when we simply add fresh ingredients such as garlic, ginger and onions, or expose them to the sunlight for a while.

Exercise and breathing techniques increase these energies, and so does spending time in the outdoors, in a park, on the countryside and especially in forests.

Meditation works very well too and yes, sleeping is another great way to re-energize ourselves.

But let's move on and look how the ethereal energy connects with other energy levels. And how it serves as an important link between mind and body.

The old cultures of India, China, the Hopi Indians of America, the Australian Aborigines and others talk about seven main transformation points of energy in our bodies. These energy wheels, 'Chakras' or 'Dan Tiens' correspond in the physical body with the endocrine glands.

Energy is transformed either upwards or downwards; the vibration levels are increased or decreased. An exchange of energy and information takes place. The process is quite similar to electricity where the power station needs to gradually decrease the voltage in substations. A factory needs higher voltage than household appliances. And the battery in a car uses again lower voltage, all the way down to children's toys.

Energy flows and the created energy fields always follow the laws of mutual induction and resonance. These laws can be easily observed in the field of electricity and the overtones and octaves of music, but again, they apply universally.

The electricity of a power line may jump onto a parallel line of wires where we hang up our clothes during days of high humidity. This mutual induction causes electrons to flow in the wire and may give us a small electric shock when they discharge through our body to the earth. That's static electricity. And who has not had the uncomfortable experience of touching a door handle on a cold and dry day?

Energy is constantly moving and it affects its surroundings to various degrees. And it always strives to maintain the natural balance again, somehow and somewhere.

Everything is inter-connected, without exceptions. There is nothing that exists without having an effect on the rest of the energies making up the universe. This is true within the billions of cells of our bodies and ultimately, all our interactions with the external world. The gravity field of the moon for example, effects the tides of our oceans.

And when it can influence these vast quantities of water, it is not surprising that it also affects our body and mind. Statistics show an increased number of accidents and violent incidents on full-moon nights just to name another example.

More and more people become increasingly aware of the interconnection between All That Is, and its constant interaction.

REALIZATION 22 ~ 25

•

All energy flows create an energy field!

•

Everything is connected with each other!

•

Energy of similar wave length resonate together!

•

Similar energies attract each other!

•

The last frontier

You have surely heard the age old question. What came first, the chicken or the egg?

Sorry guys, I can't give you that answer. Why? Well, it's a secret! Just kidding. No, I don't really know the answer, but suspect it to be the egg.

Is the body influencing the mind? Sure. Just have a couple of drinks too many and you know!

Is the mind influencing our bodies? Of course. We think of making a certain move and our bodies follow. Quite easy under normal circumstances. But when our minds become clouded up by too many beers, well, our bodies become a lot harder to control.

The better we learn to coordinate mind and body and vice versa, the less effort we need to make. It is quite obvious that our bodies and minds constantly influence each other.

Breathing exercises help us to calm down when our mind is racing and relax the body at the same time. When we think and analyze a lot of complex problems, our bodies will feel exhausted, too. We may get shoulder tension and a stiff neck.

Some scientists consider the mind to be the last frontier, because there are still many unknowns challenging the analytical mind.

In more recent years aura photography has been developed, where the electromagnetic fields generated by the various electrical impulses in the body are made visible. These new aura pictures go beyond the ethereal level and show the even more subtle energy fields, such as the ones created by our mind and emotions.

The colorful pictures generated are then used in many holistic treatments for diagnosis and observing the achieved improvements.

As you know now, the different auras are generated by the flow of different energies vibrating at different velocity or wave lengths. And remember that all happens *simultaneously in the same space*.

There are quite many places these days where you can

have pictures taken of your aura. Try it at different times and in different physical, mental and emotional conditions. Without the need to be an expert, you will easily see quite a difference in your aura pictures.

Brain waves are generating the subtle mind aura. And it is also interacting constantly with the various energy fields of our physical body via the chakras.

Ultimately the interaction expands to everything else in the universe. And to everybody else, too!

Does your mind aura become influenced by somebody else's? Yes. But it goes both ways. And obviously a mentally stronger person has a deeper impact on a weaker person, and vice versa.

Have you noticed how new friends suddenly start to use the same expressions, both language and body language? When you move to another country with a totally different culture you will see how strongly you will become influenced. Even a person who moves to a different state in a particular country will change some speech and behavior patterns.

Increasingly, we become aware that our well-being is influenced to a large degree by our mind. *Well-balanced, strong and happy people have a stronger immune system and get less affected by sicknesses.*

Disharmony in the energy field of one particular vibration level will influence negatively the energy fields of all other levels, while harmony, too, is expanding to benefit our total being. The word 'dis-ease' explains itself very well. When we are not at ease in our mind, we can become physically sick, too.

So whenever we are happy, we are obviously at ease with ourselves. And therefore we feel well in the sum total of our being. *Being happy is all we need to be. It is the best medicine!*

We exist in various dimensions at the same time and we can become increasingly aware of them as we expand our sensitivity.

REALIZATION 26~27

•

I am multi-dimensional!

•

I desire harmony in everything!

•

The Dan Tien Tao

Here I would like to introduce you to a great and pleasant exercise. It is a very old Chinese Tao, or internal Kung Fu system and is called the 'mysterious Dan Tien Tao'.

Once through, you will feel energized and very refreshed! It balances our chi and increases our sensitivity for the more subtle energies of our self.

The titles that follow are the exact translation of the original Chinese text. That is all that was ever written down and as you will see, it is very short and doesn't make much sense. Traditionally, ancient knowledge was jealously guarded. The secrets were handed down from generation to generation, either within a family or among the monks and nuns in monasteries.

Anybody who somehow got the written encoded text would not know what it was for or how it was used. A master passing it on to a trusted student, shows such a Tao in great detail in private closed door meetings only. And the old text, which may never be changed, serves only as a reminder.

When I met the master of a Buddhist monastery on the Sun Moon lake in central Taiwan, he told me that now he has to give me something. I don't know why he felt that way. For decades he has not shown the mysterious Dan Tien Tao to anybody, not even to his fellow monks.

All he knew about me, was that I was a Kung Fu student, vegetarian (at that time) and interested in the deeper aspects of life. He just served some tea, showed me how it is done properly, gave me the original text and that was it. I never met him again and I was quite puzzled until I started to write this book.

Did he somehow know that I would someday write a book and pass on this knowledge to a wider audience?

He said: "In winter, you will never feel cold and in summer, you will never feel hot".

What was very striking with the master is that, although he was in his eighties, his skin was smooth and looked almost baby-like. And his general appearance and strength would make a lot of guys in their mid-forties jealous!

He recommended doing the exercise after waking up or before sleeping, while still in bed. And yes, you have to be naked while doing it. Maybe that's why he didn't teach it to his Buddhist students who sleep all together in dormitories!

It works so well that I would do it only in the mornings, otherwise I wouldn't be able to sleep anymore. The instructions may look rather funny at first sight.

But try it for week or two, every day, and decide for yourself how well it works for you!

1. Section: *Upper Dan Tien*

1. Set: *"Three knocks of the heavenly drum and seven knocks of the holy bell"*

Push the under side of the tongue all the way upwards. Now pull it down suddenly together with the lower jaw. It produces a sound from the 'vacuum effect' and it will get louder as you improve this with some practice. Do it three times.

Hit very gently both ears at the same time with both palms. The palms are soft and relaxed, forming a little bowl. The mouth is totally opened and we exhale softly, continuously and completely. Do this seven times, all in one go.

2. Set: *"Two military regiments march on the mountain"*
From now on **through the entire exercise, before starting each set,** rub both palms for a while until they feel hot, pulsating with energy. The only exception is Section 3, set 2.

With the tips of both hands tap gently and quickly on your head, **until you feel the heat.**

Start at the forehead and move slowly backwards, all the way down to the neck. Do it also sidewards down to the ears while starting at the top of the head.

3. Set: *"Ten officers defend the five closed gates"*
Close the eyes and mouth, inhale fully and hold your breath (just during this third set please!). Strike with all ten fingers from the hairline down the face and over the throat. Do it until you feel the heat.

4. Set: *"The green dragon flies out in all directions"*
Push out your tongue as much as you can and as straight as you can. Now make complete circles, as round as possible, with the tongue as much extended as you can. 24 times in both directions. Swallow the saliva; it's good for you.

2. Section: *Middle Dan Tien*

1. Set: *"Five tigers coming from the mountain and running 36 circles"*
Strike firmly with the left hand down the side of the right arm, starting from the shoulder all the way to the finger tips. Do it 36 times. And then again on the left arm with your right hand.

2. Set: *"Sun and moon run nine circles with the ten heavenly poles"*
Massage the right chest with your left hand. First nine times clockwise, then ten times anti clockwise.

And then the same way on the left chest with your right hand.

3. Set: *"Twelve reasons support the heat in the oven"*
Massage the stomach with the fingers of both hands. Start from the centre, both ring fingers on the navel, and strike simultaneously to both sides. Do it twelve times.

4. Set: *"East and West, two cities are meeting four villages"*
Massage the lower stomach with both hands, without using the thumbs. Again start at the centre, both pointing fingers just below the navel, and strike simultaneously to both sides. Do it until you feel the heat.

3. Section: *Lower Dan Tien*

1. Set: *"The moving of three sheep to the southern and northern border"*
Massage with the three middle fingers of both hands downwards until you reach the genitals. This is the remaining area which wasn't covered by the previous two sets. Start again at the centre, strike downwards. Then do it everywhere on both sides, always downwards, moving towards the left and the right. Until you feel the heat.

2. Set: *"Four soldiers united to attack the end of the centre"*
Make two fists; bring the knuckles together. Now extend the middle finger and the ring finger of each hand, keeping the other fingers clenched. When the fingernails are touching (ring to ring, middle to middle), and you look at them from the top (the finger-tips), you will see a square made up of the four finger-tips. Move this 'square', behind your back, to the very beginning of your spine. Push up very gently several times until you feel the heat.

3. Set: *"The heavenly poles are running thirty-six circles on the left and on the right"*
Strike firmly with the right hand down on the side of the right leg, starting from the hip all the way down over the

ankle. Do it 36 times. And then again on the left leg with your left hand. Until you feel the heat.

4. Set: *"Yin and Yang meet 108 times"*
Massage the underside of the left foot with the lower palm of the right hand. Strike from the heel until you reach the toes. Do it 108 times. And finally, do the same on your right foot with your left hand.

You did it! And remember that with regular practice, you will improve the results. After doing it a few times you will easily remember how it's done.

It takes about fifteen to twenty minutes, depending on whether you are in a hurry or not. Take your time and use it to wake up slowly and nicely.

Rewinding the clock

Meditation has been practiced for thousands of years and has now become increasingly popular in the western countries, too. The positive effects on mind and body are well known. It relieves us of stress and tensions. It replenishes energy, restores harmony and our natural sensitivity.

There are many techniques to choose from and we can find out what works best for us.

I like simple, effective and comfortable ways, without any rules or regulations attached.

The first goal is to calm down the mind and thereby relax the body. When too many thoughts race through our mind we can sit or lay down in a comfortable position, close the eyes and concentrate on our breathing.

Just breathe out the air naturally and wait for the instinctive urge to inhale. It's like an ignition spark. When inhaling, the stomach area should lift up first, then the ribs area and finally the chest area. And when we feel like exhaling, we should do it in the same order. The stomach area deflates first, followed by the ribs and chest area.

It should all be natural and relaxed. The more our breathing becomes relaxed, the deeper it gets while the rhythm slows down. And as it becomes slower and deeper, less and less thoughts go through our mind. We can enjoy feeling good, being relaxed, comfortable and secure, ask questions, see answers, concentrate on a project or dream, seeing it become a reality, or fall asleep and wake up refreshed, whatever we like.

We can meditate in bed before sleeping at night and in the morning before getting up. Or while walking in the park, breathing deeply and enjoying the beauty of nature. We can meditate while taking a shower or taking a hot bath. In can be brief or long, it doesn't matter, as long as we feel good.

We can be in a meditative state of mind all the time when we are mindful of every moment as discussed previously. When every moment becomes meaningful, every action thoughtful, time seems to slow down. There is no more rushing through life or experiencing sensations of stress. ***The world starts to increasingly move at our own pace.***

One way which works very well is when we breathe and/or meditate as above, and combine it with the sound vibrations of the chakras. Sound has power as it is vibrating energy. We all know the effect music has on our mind and behavior. Department stores and supermarkets use stimulating background music because it increases the sales.

Research with classical music showed an improvement in the intellectual abilities of those students who listened to it, compared with others who didn't. Hard Rock had a negative effect on students. The same results were obtained in experiments with plants.

The energy vibration of each chakra resembles a particular sound. These sounds have a balancing and cleansing effect on the chakra energies.

Once we are already in a happy mindset, we don't need to think about our chakras. Whether the energies are in harmony and balanced or not, because everything adjusts automatically. But on the way there, you may find this exercise very helpful as it completely relaxes our body and mind.

Give it a go and enjoy yourself!

Take a deep breath and exhale on the first word, LAM. Say it loud in a comfortable volume. Do it several times, as often as you like. Then exhale with the sound vibration of the second chakra, VAM. Just vibrate each letter as you exhale slowly, until you run out of air.

LLLLLLLLLAAAAAAAAAMMMMMMMMM.
VVVVVVVVAAAAAAAAMMMMMMMM.
RRRRRRRRAAAAAAAAAMMMMMMMMM.
YYYYYYYAAAAAAAAAMMMMMMMM.
HHHHHHHHHAAAAAAAAAMMMMMMMM.
AAAAAAAUUUUUUUUMMMMMMMM.

Repeat each one about the same times, say five to ten times each. Do it all the way through the six sound vibrations.

At the end, try to link them all together, every word just once, in a single breath. And repeat it several times.

It is quite amazing to realize that this exercise works even when you do this quietly in your mind only... And you can increase the effects when, while inhaling, you imagine the respective sounds, too.

R E A L I Z A T I O N   2 8

•

I can meditate to relax and expand myself!

•

CHAPTER 6

Relationship Matters

Happy communications

Now it's time to look at many practical applications of the previously discussed. No more theory. Big promise!

Let's see first how we can improve our communications. Our social life doesn't need to be unpleasant at all. We can have a good time with other folks, all the time! To a very wide degree, it is up to us...

We interact with the outside world by talking, with body language, in writing and by our thoughts. And these are, as everything else, energy vibrations. Higher energy or lower energy, depending on our own condition, strength and intentions. *All of our communication has an internal effect on us. And external effect on our environment, both animate and inanimate.*

Kind words are a lot more pleasant to hear and speak than an angry exchange of words. Words can soothe or hurt, be uplifting or depressing. The result may be immediate or delayed in time.

The energy waves we send out, reflect back on us and create changes in our lives. It is similar to the echo effect, which echoes back our words when we shout in the mountains. At worst, the vibrating sound waves of our yelling could start an avalanche, moving hundreds of tons of snow.

Of course, not all of our communication need to result in such a dramatic reaction. Often we don't even notice the effects of our words consciously. But that doesn't mean that there is no effect.

A guy I knew for many years had the habit of constantly making remarks like: "He is such a pain in the a...!" or "This is such a pain in the a...!"

Are you surprised to hear that over all these years he suffered badly of hemorrhoids? Is it just a coincidence?

"This is really sickening!", "He makes me sick!", "What a stress!", "It drives me crazy!", "I'm going insane!", "What a crazy world!", "It's terrible!", "It gives me a headache!", "I could kill him!", "I'd die for an ice cream now!".

What kind of message do we send out by such words? What results can we expect to reap for our bodies and mind? What kind of reality are we creating for ourselves? Anything desirable? I'm pretty sure that you know the answer already...

Keeping all our communications and expressions positive and precise has a very uplifting effect. We can always say things clearly and in a positive way and it will help us tremendously.

Once you make the conscious decision to watch your language, you will notice more, how often people use negative language. Or how often you used to... When you ask people in Australia how they are, the most common answer you will hear is: "Not too bad!"

Well, they may truly feel that way and say so. I suspect however, that very often, it is an automatic answer. A customary habit and not an actual expression of how they feel at that point in time.

"Not too bad" means not too good either, but people say so often while at a party and obviously enjoying themselves.

In the United States you will hear so often the exact opposite. When you ask people there you will hear: "Absolutely terrific!", "Just splendid!", "Awesome!", "Fantastic!", "Absolutely wonderful!".

The problem is only that they often don't look or feel like that at all! You may observe somebody with a sour face. And the whole body language is one of sorrows, anger or worries. But still, when you approach the person and ask, you will hear a very positive response.

Although, when you consider the amazing popularity of positive thinking books in the last few years, it is perhaps less surprising.

When I talk about using positive and powerful expressions, I don't propose to paint over grey pictures with rosy colors. Not at all! All you need to do is *express your personal reality and do it in a positive way.*

Never say, "I'm feeling great", when you actually feel lousy. It will not make your situation or your true feelings any better at all. On the contrary.

By doing so you are saying that you are happy with circumstances that you are not really happy about. Your desire is to be happy and feel great.

So if an unhappy situation comes into your life, but you keep on saying that you feel great, then you will just get more of the same.

And that's not what you want! Right? It is very important to acknowledge your reality as it is. And to know how to change it.

How you can create your own reality, the one you desire from the bottom of your heart.

Don't just hang around, feeling miserable and then say: "I feel great!" This will not only *not* change that miserable reality. But ensure that it continues to be miserable ...

So it is far better that you admit a temporary setback, without complaining. It is not shameful or embarrassing to admit the truth. Everybody has sometimes a temporary setback .

But to say that you feel so great when the other person can obviously tell that it isn't so, well, that is embarrassing!

"I have got a problem to deal with right now, but it will be ok. I will do my best!"

"This situation is not what I want but I will make the best out of it!", "I've got a bit of a problem right now, but I can handle it!" In truly bad situations you may say: "Oh well, it can only get better from now on!", "I've got a few problems. Could surely use some help!" And you might get it!

Whenever you feel truly great, then you should say so and invite more of that into your life. Because that is what you want. Feel great!

You will send out the message to all the atoms and energies, both within and without: "Yes! That feels great. That's exactly what I want!" And you welcome more of that.

It is not necessary to fully open up yourself to strangers.

But be precise. Say you feel ok, but you know that you can feel a lot better. So you can say: "Pretty good!" or "OK!"

If something is troubling you, and yet you can stay centered and still be happy within, say something like: "Pretty good considering this or that!" or "Could be better right now. Thanks for asking!"

Be honest about it, brief, and always end on a positive note. "A bit upset right now. Anyway, at least the sun is shining!" Enjoy the sunshine and point it out. Thereby you will communicate that you are in charge of your life and mood. And not about to complain about this or that for the next ten minutes!

When we say: "Don't forget!", it is a double negative. "Not" and "forget". And people may hear this with the emphasis on "Forget". And then, surprise, surprise, they do forget!

Put in a positive way, all we need to say is: "Remember!" Chances are a lot better that a person reminded in this way will actually remember!

Or say more: "I can do it" rather than "I can't do it." There is a lot more that we can do than we often think. All we need is a bit of confidence and the will to try and succeed!

If there is something that you don't want to do when somebody asks you, it would be better to say:

"I don't want to do it", "I don't like doing this", or "It is important that I finish doing this now." If you say "I have no time to do it", it sends out the wrong signal too because we have time.

Just consider how many hours a day are spent watching TV...

Instead of saying lightly: "It's impossible!" we can say, "I will give it a try!" or "I will do my best!" Every time we say: "I don't know", it sends a weakening message to our subconscious mind.

More often than not, we know what to do. Or we can easily find out the best course of action *by listening within.*

Remember our best friend?

A better way is to say: "I don't know about this", because there are things that you do know, or "I don't know yet." You have the confidence that you will know what to do, when the time has come.

We should make an effort and keep our total communication as precise as possible. And we will benefit greatly.

Just think for a moment how many misunderstandings you had with other people. And how often it was because you didn't make things very clear. So many potential arguments can be easily avoided, and all the tears that accompany them...

Have you noticed how often some people waste time with gossiping and badmouthing? It is not just a waste of time but an unnecessary negative interaction. There is always an exchange of bad energies taking place, pulling us down.

When we talk bad about other people we build a mental connection to these people. More precisely, to the negative energy fields created by their emotions – the darker part of their beings, where all the stress, sadness, anger and depression is hidden quietly. You may or may not be consciously aware of this reality, nevertheless, that's what happens anyway. And it has effects on you. Sooner or later...

To tap into these pools of negativity is not an enjoyable affair. It doesn't feel good. And it is not a source of happiness.

Who has not experienced the fact that ultimately, the person talked about will hear all those things we said? Besides, when we keep company with people who gossip all the time, what are they saying about us when we are not present?

My policy is to concentrate on the positive aspects of people, whether they are present or not.

It feels really good to talk well about somebody. That's how you build a connection to their positive pool of energies, to all their good qualities, abilities and achievements.

Watch what happens in a discussion where people tend to talk negatively about others. Usually the one talked about is not present, of course. Now say some good stuff about the person. Suddenly others will say some positive things, too, while the really negative people will have nothing to contribute anymore. It literally shuts them up! It's an easy and effective way to change the direction of a discussion. And it injects positive energies again. Besides, when you talk well about people and they hear about it, they will certainly not send negative and destructive vibes your way!

If you really don't know anything positive to say, than it is better to just keep quiet. But as you increase your happiness, you will find it very easy to always say something positive. It happens very naturally!

You can always change the topics of a conversation. Since you are focused on beauty and happiness, you will notice things others may not see at the time.

"Oh, look it's a full moon night. Wow, it's so beautiful!" In a worst case scenario you can always leave and find greener pastures somewhere else.

Better being happy alone than keeping company with people who stick to a die-hard, negative frame of mind.

Often gossip is centered around matters of taste. "She wears too much make up!", "What an ugly dress!", "Look at him, he is such a show off!"

The individual sense of taste is really nothing worth arguing about. There is no good or bad taste. It is a personal choice and we should respect that. Taste is often a country- or culture-specific thing. And ultimately, each person's decision of what makes him/her feel good.

There is a fine line between gossiping and exchanging information. If you talk about your personal experience with somebody and you keep it neutral, it is not going to affect you. You simply state a fact, without the urge to inject some unnecessary emotional smog.

"I did business with him last year. And unfortunately, he didn't honor his side of the deal. I don't know why, but I was pretty disappointed!"

Notice how often successful and happy people use powerful, precise and positive expressions in their private and professional lives. It is not a coincidence. The classical example is: "The glass is already half empty," versus "the glass is still half full." It is our choice.

Using positive and precise communication will help us to be more happy because it sends out the right energy, to ourselves, to everybody, and to everything!

We know now that thoughts are more subtle energy waves than spoken or written words. And they too interact, reflect, and cause effects. Not just within our overall being, but externally, as well.

The external world as we perceive it, has its origin within. Remember that the micro-and macro-cosmos are mirroring each other.

As you reduce stress within yourself, you will notice that the world around you has somehow slowed down, too. And that there are suddenly less stressful events showing up in your life!

It is quite ironic sometimes. When you already feel stressed out within your mind, all of a sudden all these problems seem to show up, too, and make things worse, and you feel like, "Oh no. Everything/everybody is against me!"

When you feel less sad or mad within, the world becomes suddenly a brighter place than before. There will be less sad events in your life. And less reasons to become angry.

And as you increase your feelings of happiness within, you will have less and less serious problems to deal with. More and more opportunities for your enjoyment will start to materialize... Anytime and anywhere. And suddenly, all the time!

So watch and control your thoughts, and guide them in a more positive and constructive direction.

Whenever we observe dark thoughts going through the

mind, we can choose to either completely immerse in that thought, maybe getting more and more angry, sad or outright depressed. Or we can just notice it and decide to not follow it up any further. Dismiss negative thoughts by exhaling deeply, letting them go away.

And consciously decide to change the direction towards more pleasant thoughts. Remember all the happy moments and possibilities that are just waiting for you to enjoy...

We can all do this if we want to. It is a process which may take a bit of time and practice. But it is an effort well worth making!

REALIZATION 29 ~ 32

•

I always express myself positively!

•

I express myself clearly and precisely!

•

I concentrate on positive thoughts!

•

I speak only positively about people!

•

Nothing but the truth

To clearly say what you mean and do so positively is only part of the magic formula. To also mean what we say, makes it complete. For the same reasons as above and more, it is equally important to ***always speak the truth.***

We have to know that our word counts. And that everybody else knows it, too. Lies have a tendency to turn back on us. And we know now that they send out the wrong messages both to ourselves and to our environment.

Besides, we feel bad about lying, at least in our subconscious. And sooner or later we will have to face the music...

It is amazing that once you fully trust your word because you always honor it, others will trust you, too, even if they have never met you before or heard about you. ***Once you always speak the truth, your words have automatic authority. Think about that for a minute and what this means for your Plan...***

People who often lie, also lie to themselves, even if they are not aware of it. Liars cheat mostly themselves and can not realize or attract lasting happiness into their lives. They make the wrong decisions at the wrong times. And they are often in the wrong places at the wrong time.

Being truthful also means to keep our promises. If we are not sure that we can or will keep a promise, it is better to not make such a pledge. Better no promise than an empty one.

As always we should start quietly with our self. When I pledge to myself that I will finish something by today, I should be straight with myself and actually do it today. No excuses allowed.

This will give us more strength and a lot of self-confidence. And it simply feels good...

Others will notice our strong sense of integrity, too, and will know that they can rely on us.

Ultimately this will not just lead us to a more harmonious and pleasant understanding with people, but to greater wealth, as well...

One way to practice this in a small but important way is to always be on time.

When you make an appointment at two p.m., be there at two p.m. You don't need to be early either, just on time. It is not that hard to achieve once you have made up your mind.

If you are not sure about your timing, that's OK, as long as you don't make any commitment. We can state that we can not be exactly sure about when we will get there, and suggest to the other party to please wait in a coffee shop instead of a street corner. This small move is a great exercise and will certainly be received positively by everybody around you.

Of course, there are situations where we don't want to reveal everything about our life and plans openly. Maybe we don't trust a particular person after some bad experiences. Or our intuition tells us that we can't trust somebody, without knowing the reasons why. In business matters, we have to be diplomatic at times. Or maybe we just want to avoid becoming a subject in the local gossip club.

Nevertheless, in all these situations we can still speak the truth. There is no need to lie, even so-called white lies. Look, we can always tell just part of the story...

If we reveal just say, five percent out of the total picture, there is no harm done at all. Small bits of information will reveal nothing really. They can be actually quite misleading. And yet, it satisfies curious people.

It is far better to reveal a little bit of information and stay in control of the general direction than being suddenly faced with outrageous rumors further down the road. And here comes another great benefit of always speaking the truth: ***We know automatically whenever somebody lies to us, or tries to cheat us!*** So now, we can simply walk away from such people and their proposals. It gives us an invaluable edge in both private and business relationships, anytime we interact with people in any way. And it saves us from a lot of unnecessary troubles, headaches and heartaches.

You will see very easily through the attempts of people trying to appear better, stronger, smarter or wealthier than they really are. Some people even put others down in order to appear more favorably.

But any kind of pretending will only fool those people who also fool themselves. ***The truth just is. Always. It is that simple.*** And any manipulation of the truth, in whatever form and shape it may appear, will still not change it.

Being always truthful with our self and others has only advantages. It is like taking a huge shortcut on our path to ever-increasing happiness.

So let's love the truth, live the truth, feel the truth. All the time!

REALIZATION 33 ~ 34

•

I always communicate the truth!

•

My word is good as gold!

•

The ultimate desire

Have you ever wondered what makes us all tick? What is it that we all want very badly, regardless of where we were born or under what circumstances? No matter what color our skin is or to what God we pray to, if any.

Yes, we all want to eat nice food, dress in good-looking clothes and live in a comfortable place we can call home. But apart from this, we all share something more profound. It is quite simply this:

We all want to feel accepted. We all desire to be respected. And we are all craving to be loved.

This original desire is one of the universal characteristics we all have in common.

Some people may consider themselves to be rational, and the above-mentioned desires to be irrational or even silly. Yet, they also share them with everybody else. They may just not be aware of it... So, how rational are we humans anyway?

As much as some people think we humans are different from animals because of our ability to think, analyze and rationalize, as little is this true. It is really just a big illusion. Or delusion perhaps...

Let's consider a few examples. How rational is it to pollute the water we all need to drink? The air we all need to breathe? Or otherwise destroy and exploit nature in an unsustainable way? To be greedy is one thing, but to spoil your own nest is quite another. Not exactly the logical thing to do, is it?

And how rational is it to pay twenty times the price of the exact same T-shirt just because it bears a particular name or logo? I have visited factories in China and been an avid shopper of designer goods myself. It is quite different if you pay a lot more for a product that is really superior in quality and design than a much cheaper one. But often they are just the same thing being produced in the exact same place...

Let's say you drive around in an old rusty VW Beetle. Would you park it right in front of a 'mega-trendy' restaurant? And where would you try to park your car when a friend lends you his brand new Ferrari for the night?

Why do we feel better when we surround ourselves with status symbols of all kinds?

Or why do sport events become so emotionally charged that they can at times spin totally out of control? When people identify themselves with one or the other party, they can take victory or defeat very, very personally. If somebody's favorite team wins, what did that person contribute anyway, except lot's of noise perhaps, where the player needed extra energy to keep up his or her concentration?

There is so much idol worship going on, for pop stars, royalty, models or sport icons. Even the odd politician here and there.

What makes some people look up to others like that, desiring guidance and a meaning for themselves? It is nice to be inspired by successful people. There is no doubt about that. But idol worship is quite another matter. Why do some people look to others for feelings of self-worth?

Powerful politicians want to be respected, admired and finally, remembered. Preferably, in a positive light of course.

Even a brutal dictator wants to be loved by somebody. They may induce fear in most of their subjects, but cling to the love and adoration of a woman, perhaps. Or their mother. Somebody, anyway.

Wealthy people often get their satisfaction not from the fact that they are rich and live in comfortable surroundings. There are not that many people who are rich in a quiet way. Part of the satisfaction is to let others know of their fortunes. And get their due admiration, respect, and envy.

There are relatively few donations given or charities performed anonymously, for the same reasons.

How much satisfaction do you get from giving away money if only the tax man knows about it?

Throughout my life I have met people from all walks of life. I have worked side by side with the 'working class' and later on, dined side by side with the 'movers and shakers'.

The more or less beautiful, the more or less rich, the more or less powerful. And I realized that we are pretty much the same in so many respects. We are a lot less rational than we often think we are...

Subjective reasons can be the prime motivation for people to go out into the world and do things. And this innermost desire is **very** often the basis of our decision making.

This is reality. And it is a good reality for as long as we can improve our happiness.

It is one thing to realize what makes us tick. But now, let's now look at some of the pitfalls. And draw the right conclusions...

The strong

Some people seem to be so self-confident at first sight. They may be very successful and possess all the external symbols of success. Often they are considered to be winners in our society and they stand out for their competitive drive. They always want to win, no matter what and where, even in a harmless game with friends and family. And usually, if they lose, they are poor losers.

If it were only to advance in life and become comfortably established from a material point of view, how come they cannot stop after they have already achieved these goals?

Could it be that they actually lack true self-esteem? That they haven't learned to respect themselves? That they don't really accept and love themselves, and so, they have to continuously prove to themselves that they are worth something?

The problem is that such attempts of convincing themselves through external means doesn't work.

To receive confirmation of something that is not real will not make us happy. It is as simple as that. Illusions bring only very fleeting moments of joy...

Competitive winner types ultimately learn it the hard way that their lifestyle brings with it a lot of opposition, jealousy and hatred. In other words, bad energy.

More often than not, they are not very popular, and without many true friends, if any at all.

And life on the top can become very lonely. The lonely wolf. Just the opposite of what they really wanted to achieve deep within themselves...

So very often, the strong are actually not that strong at all, because their strength is not real, but rather wishful thinking! They may think that they are very important and irreplaceable. They can come across in aggressive and intimidating ways, or arrogant.

Some have really convinced themselves that they are smart and always right, better than others. Worth more. Deserving to be on the top and looking down on the "ordinary" or "common" folks. It is quite amazing that some seem to truly believe such nonsense...

But no matter how strong they can come across, it is all just a big show. A lot of hot air, and not based in reality. *To project strength when there is no real strength is a very tiring affair, and most definitely an unhappy one as well!*

Anybody who really thinks himself or herself to be the salt of the Earth should look up to all the stars above, on a beautiful and clear night, in the countryside where lights don't interfere, and then say: "I'm such an important person!" That should do the trick.

And the weak

Chances are pretty good that you don't belong to the category described above. Why? Well, if you truly believed that you know everything best, you would not bother to read this book. Right?

Nevertheless, it is important to understand, not just yourself, but other people as well. What makes them behave the way they do? It is good to know how to deal with them and it will help us a lot in life.

So, what is the difference between those who appear to be strong and those who appear to be weak? Nothing really.

In terms of behavior, there is certainly a lot of difference. But from a personal energy point of view, there is no difference at all. And those who pretend less are certainly the more honest.

Think about this for a minute or so: *People who don't accept themselves are terribly eager to feel accepted by everybody else. People who don't respect themselves are terribly eager to get respected by everybody else. People who don't love themselves are terribly eager to be loved by everybody else.*

This eagerness shows in all of their communication. You will find the symptoms among the rich and poor, the more and less successful...

Too little self-acceptance, respect and love is a continuous source of unhappiness. And so is too much of it...

Feelings of loneliness and depression, abuse of both legal and illegal drugs, overeating and other self-destructive behavior are often the consequences.

Tens of millions of people in the USA alone regularly take anti-depression drugs such as Prozac, throughout all the age groups and the entire social spectrum...

People with a low sense of self-esteem easily agree with others and generally try to blend in with the way they speak, dress and behave. They are afraid of standing out. Afraid of being rejected. Afraid of confronting somebody, even after being cheated.

Desperately needing and wanting acceptance. Often they are very accommodating and have a hard time saying no. Trying too hard to please others all the time. But that is simply impossible! We can't please everybody. Somebody will always still feel disappointed and complain.

We are not here to please others and give up our own life and happiness. Some people realize this only very late in their life. How little gratitude and appreciation they have earned themselves that way anyway. Then they become increasingly bitter, dis-illusioned, frustrated, and depressed.

They forgot to seek happiness for themselves. Or did not dare to... Some of this may or may not apply to you. If it does, don't worry. We can fix it. It is a lot easier than bringing a person who is too puffed up down to reality. For such a person only very harsh experiences will bring the eventual remedy. And such experiences are bound to happen sooner or later...

Here is a good way to test whether you are self-confident or not. I call it the dance test.

How often do you go dancing? Don't tell me that you don't like music. And get used to the idea of dancing a lot from now on. It is one thing we happy people have all in common. It is, like laughing and smiling, a very natural thing to do when you are happy.

I'm not talking about the show-off type dancing where you dance in order to satisfy the desire to be recognized. Nope. Just dance and be happy. Dance because you enjoy your life. Because you feel soooooo happy and joyful....

OK. Back to the test. Some people don't like to dance because they are afraid of what other people may think of them. That they might look silly or somehow out of place. Fears like that. Can you go out and dance like nobody is watching you? And have a great time, feeling happy, and no worries are creeping up on you? None at all, even when people are staring at you?

How many people can feel so liberated and comfortable? Even when they may not be very good dancers. Check it out for yourself and visit a dancing spot.

How many people are dancing easily and happily, without any inhibitions? Look at it for a while. Look at the beautiful and the gorgeous. Those that look so self-confident when sitting down or standing at the bar. See what I mean? There is really not that much of a difference in people. Between the strong and the weak. Right?

So what is the happy solution? Yes. You guessed it right! It is simply this:

Accept yourself.

•

Respect yourself.

•

Love yourself.

That may sometimes sound easier than it is done. Deep-rooted reasons we carry around for a long, long time can at times be hard to overcome overnight. It may be due to very critical and demanding parents. Often the children of a very successful father will struggle all their lives to try and keep up with him. Maybe a lousy teacher was working overtime on our case. Or some kind of failure early in our childhood makes life still hard for us. Maybe other kids were making fun of the way you looked back then. Whatever. It is good to find out what the possible causes are. It can help us to overcome insecurity.

So find a quiet moment again and think back to your early childhood. See yourself when you were a little boy or girl.

And ask that person what hurt his/her feelings, like you would be talking to somebody else who is not you. Ask sincerely and be kind. What a lovely and sweet child! So pure and innocent. Love. And feel loved. Ask as many questions as you like and listen to the answers within.

"How can I accept and love myself when I'm so fat and ugly?" The truth is that nobody is perfectly happy with the way their body looks.

Even super models have complaints about themselves and want to be reassured. And this is entirely apart from the fact that they too like to receive compliments. Honest ones anyway. They may admit to some beautiful aspects of their faces or bodies, but none of them are 100% happy with their looks.

The nose is too flat, the breasts too big or small, legs too short or the bottom too fat. Whatever. Why are so many ladies on the "losing weight trip"? Or why is there such a high demand for cosmetic surgery, both among men and women?

I have two strong and big front teeth where 'normally' people have four. And there is a big gap in between them, too. When I was a kid, it didn't bother me at all. But as a teenager it did, and I was kind of reluctant to smile broadly because of my teeth. It is quite easy to pull them out and replace them with four artificial ones. And yet I didn't bother anyway.

I just learned to accept them the way they look. I even like them now...

Who decided anyway what beautiful is? Just consider this. There are about three billion women. And so many of them struggle to look just like a few super models. It's a bit crazy, isn't it?

Besides, the fashion industry is changing all the time. Ideal looks are changing, too. Marilyn Monroe wasn't exactly slim, was she?

Accept yourself the way you are. It is a fact that most men don't like skinny women. Some ladies like bold men, too. And so on.

There is no such thing as an ugly person. Everybody has at least some beautiful features. And, beauty is in the eye of the beholder.

Once you have made the choice and decided to focus more on everything that you find beautiful, you will notice more beautiful aspects all the time. In yourself. In others. And everywhere else.

Besides, life is not about looks. It is about feeling happy. Right? Do you know that you are totally unique? Among the six billion people out there, no one is like you. Not one. Nobody else looks like you, feels or thinks like you, talks or behaves like you do. Welcome to the world of originals!

Respect yourself. You deserve it. You have made it this far in life already. Respect what you have learned in life. What you have done, who you are. You have qualities and abilities which nobody else has among six billion people! Nobody else has gone through all the experiences you have. And you are still here.

You are one of the heroes. Maybe not world famous, but that doesn't matter anyway. ***We are all heroes.***

We have embarked on that glorious adventure called life. Sometimes it is easy and other times hard. Maybe very hard. But you are still here. Respect that.

And you are on the right track. You have your priorities

right. You want to be happy. That's why you are reading this now.

Nobody is inferior or superior to anybody else. Beliefs to the contrary are just self-delusions. ***We may have different qualities and abilities, but ultimately we all have equal worth.***

We are all unique. Without exceptions. Each one of us has a right and reason to be here. We may not understand the reasons why yet. But eventually, we all will.

There is no need to project false pictures to the external world in order to satisfy our innermost desires. There is no need to pretend to be oh so smart and strong. And so on. We don't need to put up fake barriers to feel secure and protected once we stop denying ourselves what is real, what is naturally a part of us.

Some people get false strength from a position they hold within a company. Their social status. Their bank account. All kinds of things. It is not necessary. And very counter-productive. It won't make us really happy.

That only costs us a lot of energy. Wasted energy. Besides, what happens if somehow or another that gets lost? Some people identify themselves so strongly with their job and position. And when they lose it, all seems to be lost.

Their feeling of self-respect and self-worth is gone. They feel suddenly useless, without purpose in life. It is very often a lot worse for them than the monetary loss.

Don't put yourself in a small box with one or two labels on and try to live up to them. ***Don't limit yourself. Ever. Just be. Be strong. Be real. Be happy!***

To love yourself doesn't mean standing in front of the mirror and admire yourself for hours. No. But you should not feel bad about what you see there either.

Remember that love is a true feeling coming from within. In the beginning, loving is easier when we are quiet within, with both eyes closed. Feel the eternal quiet within and there it is. Love. Feel it, embrace it, love it.

Learn to trust your true feelings within. Your best friend

will be there and guide you, hold and comfort you and be with you all the way.

All we need to do is listen and feel. Be our own authority and source of strength.

Once we truly do that, something strange is happening all of a sudden. Or not that strange, if you think about the things we discussed in the previous chapter.

The outside world will accept you, too. Respect who you are and what you are doing. What you are standing for. Your sincerity. Your inner and real strength. And you will receive love from everywhere, too, more and more often. It just happens. Easily. You don't have to do anything at all. Just be your naturally pleasant and confident self.

REALIZATION 35 ~ 37

•

I accept myself as I am!

•

I respect myself the way I am!

•

I love myself as I am!

•

Application matters

It all comes back to the basics: energy. Real strength. Everybody is chasing after it in some form or another. And too many are trying to get it from somebody else, instead of just going within themselves, where we all have the same opportunity to tap into the unlimited source and replenish our batteries.

We can all read energy. The energy of a situation, or place. Or the energy of other people.

Some do it unconsciously. But we all have the ability to do it consciously, and see what is really happening out there.

People with low self-esteem are often afraid of being alone and seek out diversions in crowded places. They tend to seek out stronger and more confident personalities as friends because it gives them some sense of security. The security and strength they deny themselves,

Whenever people meet and interact together, there is always an exchange of energy taking place.

A person passes on some of his/her strength to the weaker. Did you notice that, whenever you are in the company of some good friends, you feel refreshed and joyful? And you could go on forever. In contrast, after meeting someone else, you feel low in energy and a bit depressed. And all you want to do is take a rest.

It is not necessary to become affected by the negative energies of other people. And we don't need to be afraid to pass on positive and strong energies. You already know where you can always get more. We will soon discuss these issues a lot more.

Positive energy that is transferred to a person will not last. It can give only a temporary boost. But when we are not living in that particular state of energy, it will quickly fade away. Nobody can hang onto positive energy if they are not living a positive energy life.

These energy transfusions are felt by the stronger party either consciously or subconsciously, and ultimately, that person doesn't like to hang around for a long time. At some point, such a person may either leave or start to exploit the other, in whatever shape and form the exploitation game is played out. Mostly it is centered around money and sex. Others are drawn like magic to hang around and worship guru types who have mastered a certain level of energetic understanding. They give up their individual right to choose. And their happiness becomes remote controlled by the whims of the puppet master.

Let's look briefly how a con man is tricking their weaker victims. It is always working a bit in the same modus operandi.

The first phase is to rob a person of the little confidence they have in the first place. Putting somebody down by criticizing a person directly or indirectly, by ridiculing their dreams and aspirations.

"No. That's not going to work!", "You don't know how to do that!", "If that idea was so smart, somebody else would have done it already!", "You are a bit silly. It's not as easy as you think!". Sound familiar?

Such people can come across more or less strongly. Then phase two starts as they build up his/her authority as the trusted advisor. The motherly, fatherly or well-meaning friend. "Trust me and all will be fine", that kind of stuff.

"Come under my wings, dear, and I will protect you, or help you, or save you!" The problem is only that it may not always be that well-meaning and selfless type of help.

You know. "Trust me!" said the cat to the mouse... In Phase Three, they will offer some solutions, some help and, you guessed it right, charge for it too, one way or another. It will cost you. Sometimes big time. "You have to do this!", "You should do it this way", "I will help you although I haven't got a lot of time!"

Once the victim's independent strength is gone, when doubts are racing through their mind, he or she will be eagerly looking for strength and guidance in the self-confident expert.

You already know the solution to the problem. But be aware of this game anyway. Be aware that some people like to use and abuse others. And some like to be used and abused, unconsciously of course.

Don't belong to either group. As you increase your strength, other people may want to increasingly depend on you. It is a new ball game and therefore important to know the name of the game, with all its rules, to ensure that you will stay away from the pitfalls. And stay happy. All the time.

At times you may still feel weak. So recognize the way confidence tricksters work. Whether they are aware of it consciously or not, doesn't really matter.

Keep your Plan to yourself. Especially when you don't feel very confident about it yet. New projects, dreams and aspirations are better kept close to your heart.

Have you ever told a close personal friend your intimate plans and then heard only negative responses? How did it feel?

More or less devastating. And maybe you suddenly didn't even feel like attacking your new project, or keeping a particular resolution, because all the enthusiasm you built up is gone. All the drive and energy disappeared with it!

This game is often played without bad intentions in mind at all. It can happen with a close and true friend. Or even a parent. And they may truly believe their objections, having your best interests at heart.

There may be some jealousy involved or some fear of changes that might affect them somehow. Maybe they are skeptics because they would not have the confidence to go through with your ambitious plan themselves. And now they project their own insecurity into your plan.

You don't want that to happen. Not to your Plan, your innermost desires. No way!

As you become stronger, it won't really matter that much anymore. Because you know that you will succeed. And nothing or nobody can stop you!

You will know to even turn around their skeptic energies

and actually make them work on behalf of your Plan...

Exploitation and coercion will always backfire, sooner or later. Truly strong and confident personalities know that they can achieve anything they want to without pushing and exploiting others. **Be strong and confident. Trust in your instincts. Be your own authority.**

When we are strong and positive, help often comes along very unexpectedly. People and things just appear and help us out. Out of the blue.

In times of need, others will show up and lend us a helping hand. Not because they feel pity, but because they want to help us. They actually enjoy it! It feels good and right to them. Everybody likes to be connected to a strong and positive person. Somehow or another. When we help a strong, positive person, we connect to that person's strength and joy – and part of that positive energy becomes ours. That's how it is! Help is always out there. This is especially true when we do likewise. It is nice to be able to help out. It feels good. Sometimes, it feels great!

We don't need to go totally out of our way to help.

It is a bit like driving along the road of life, following our Plan, whistling or singing all the way. And we see someone standing on the side of the road, asking for a lift. Well, why not?

To help someone, if it feels right, always makes us feel even better. Especially so when we do it without any hidden motives. Someday, we may need some help and it will just be there, too. Nice.

Once my wife and I drove back to LA coming from Van Nuys airport. We were a bit tired from taking flying lessons the whole day. Suddenly, a car overtook us and a few guys were shouting and gesturing very aggressively at us. They stopped in front of our car in the middle of the street and we had no other choice but to stop too. Then they got out of their car and walked towards us with grim, menacing faces.

We were quite perplexed and I was pondering whether I should get out, too, or drive on regardless of their presence in front of our car. I wasn't very thrilled with our options.

Trying to talk to them peacefully might not work, the way the situation looked. Getting into a fight might be difficult to say the least, especially in a country where people carry guns and knives. To keep driving and risk running them over, didn't sound too good either, being a foreigner in a country where litigations are easy and plentiful.

Suddenly, a pickup truck stopped besides our car. Two big and strong looking fellows started to yell at these guys. Something like: "Leave them alone or...!" They were about to get out of their car, too.

The two big men were quite convincing, and the other guys returned to their car very quickly and everybody continued their ways.

How grateful we were to our unknown friends who helped us without hesitation or any obvious motive!

When help comes our way, we shouldn't feel too proud and simply accept it. It is a great experience!

R E A L I Z A T I O N   3 8 ~ 4 0

•

I cannot be exploited!

•

I don't need to exploit others!

•

I help others and accept their help!

•

Great company

We just talked about giving and receiving help. What makes us meet people anyway? Coincidence?

You have surely come across many different kinds of people at different stages of your life. Only few people hang out with the same people all the time. Why do we change some of our friends over time? The answer lies again within ourselves.

We can tell a lot about ourselves by looking at the people we usually keep company with.

When we are often accompanied by people that complain a lot, it is because we do it, too. The complaining and unhappy energy waves resonate together and attract each other. Worse even, they reinforce each other...

So, while we are still learning to focus on being increasingly happy, it is helpful to avoid spending too much time with unhappy folks, especially the ones with particularly negative outlooks on life.

Remember that our energies resonate and interact whenever we deal with others. And usually, both parties have an effect on the other. The question is only who is influencing whom in what way, and to what degree.

As we grow up we may change some of our opinions and preferences. We may give our life a new direction and meaning. Some of our old friends and acquaintances will change with us in similar ways. And some will just fade away in a different direction. Or maybe, they are not interested in changing at all. They are comfortable where they are.

So, as our interests change, so do the people we meet and keep company with. You know the saying: "Birds of a feather flock together". It is very much true. An application of the universal law of resonance and induction. Just put a bit differently.

As we get increasingly stronger and happier, we become less and less torn and tossed around by other people and their emotions. And instead, we increase our influence on others more and more.

The strength of our positive energies will resonate with the happy potential of others. Never mind how little of that may be activated at present. It has an uplifting effect on the overall energy vibrations of people we come in contact with.

You know that when the sun is shining strongly, there is very little room for darkness left. And negative energies cannot express themselves anymore. The more we clean up our own emotions, the less such energies can have an effect on us...

Picture this: every different kind of emotion has a particular energy wave band, vibrating in a specific range of Hertz. As we reduce such negative energies within ourselves, the equivalent energies of another person will have less to resonate with, and therefore affect us and our well being less strongly.

When we have finally checked out of a particular frequency altogether, such energies will not be able to bother us at all.

We will still notice such energies because of our increased awareness of such things. We don't block out our sensitivity, but rather increase it. And yet, we can ignore negative energies easily by deciding to keep up our positive and happy mood, being centered within ourselves and connected to our source of strength.

Though the negativity of anger, jealousy, etc. may be present in a room, it has absolutely nothing to do with us. We are simply too busy being happy to let such things bother us. And we know that if that's not easily possible in one place, then we can always go someplace else!

The less negativity affects us, the stronger our happy vibrations will positively affect others. And as we get more and more happy, so will, ultimately, the happiness of the world.

You will see how you will suddenly meet more and more happy people. And make many new friends. They may come from different walks of life, from different countries and cultures with different levels of income and wealth, or with many different kind of interests. But they all have their desire to be happy in common. More and more we can share and expand our happy lifestyle together.

You will notice how some of your old friends or family members will decide to change, too, for the better...

Since the energy waves we send out will reflect back to us, we meet the people we want to meet. We will always find a resonance in people of literally similar wave lengths. All the people in our life are there for a good reason. We have invited them. And we should therefore appreciate their presence. There really is no such thing as a pure coincidence.

In the end it is up to us whether we invite the right people, or choose the right places, and circumstances to make our journey as enjoyable as we want it to be.

REALIZATION 41 ~ 42

•

I attract all the people into my life!

•

I enjoy the company of happy people!

•

Your opinion, please

Did you ever experience how a nice, civil discussion can suddenly spin out of control? Emotions and aggression start to fly. Sometimes even worse. Is that really necessary?

Opinions are too often a source of friction and arguments. How can we avoid that and stay calm and happy?

Well, the first thing we should come to realize is what they really are: *relative truths*.

They are not real and absolute truths carved forever in stone. And there are at least 600 billion opinions around the globe, if you consider each person to have only one hundred of them.

We tend to have many opinions these days. Maybe too many. And as we like to take our opinions so seriously, we forget the simple fact that they are just that – opinions. Or personal experiences. Not absolute facts.

When people used to think of the Earth as being a flat disk, they didn't really know. Maybe they thought so, but really, they just expressed an opinion. We know it better, now. But many people were put to a horrible death just because they couldn't agree.

Absolute facts are quite rare. Most facts are relative and depend on the perspective we choose. More often than not, they are based on the best knowledge or information available to us at a given time.

Let's say you are visiting Alaska for the first time. And a local Eskimo overhears you saying in the local pub: "It's so cold today!"

The Eskimo would probably be quite surprised, and disagree. It may be a particularly warm day up there and the locals enjoy it very much. And they know what it's like when temperatures are a lot lower.

What we consider to be true is just another opinion for somebody else. Think about it.

It all depends on our experiences. Our level of knowledge. Our personal interpretation of that knowledge. Our world view. Our perspectives of reality.

As we live increasingly in the information age, it becomes more and more important to learn to distinguish between opinions and facts, and to get as much information about any interesting subject from as many sources as possible. *But the most important thing to do is to check with our feelings, our best friend within.*

You may ask, what does our intuition have to do with hard and cold facts in today's world?

Well, consider this: opinions are often disguised as information. But still, they are not absolute truth or facts. ***We are living as much in the information age as we live in the misinformation age!***

Opinions are very personal, just like the individual sense of taste, and we should respect each person's right to have their own. And as we do so, we don't need to argue heatedly and condemn a person for his/her present views.

Opinions depend largely on a person's knowledge of some facts at this moment in time. This knowledge is often not complete. Then it becomes again more relative because we interlace that partial knowledge with our emotions, such as anger, fears, hopes and dreams.

Opinions are often presented as facts, but have a particular personal or political agenda hidden away somewhere. It is always good to be aware of that.

'Real' facts change less often than opinions, but facts will also change as we get smarter.

How many people live in the USA? You may look for the answer in a new edition of an encyclopedia or check with the latest government statistics. But you can be sure that the numbers given are not correct, although they appear to be. A country's population may be counted every few years. And yet, some people were not counted for various reasons. So that number was never really true. And this is beside the fact that the population figure was only a snapshot of a particular moment in time. Things change all the time. Nevertheless, the numbers given are close enough to the truth to work with.

"There are too many people living in the USA", "There are not enough people living in New Zealand." These are personal statements. In other words, opinions.

What about all the "facts" presented in history books? Consider this: history is written by the winners, often trying to justify their actions...

Did you ever come across somebody who takes his/her opinions soooooo seriously and is now totally convinced that they are fact? *Absolute* facts, for that matter! And then you will have to listen to sometimes aggressive attempts to convince you likewise. Even after pointing out that you are now aware of his/her opinion, you may hear something like: "No, this is not an opinion. This is how it is!"

These days, anybody can express their opinions to a wide audience over the Internet. And as much as I like and use the Internet, it's obvious to me how often opinions are presented as information.

So, it is good to learn to distinguish between information and misinformation. It becomes even essential if you think about how aggravating things can become. Just visit some chat rooms on the Net of any topic you care about. And see for yourself. Phew! Plenty of emotional smog around. You don't want that in your happy life. Right?

Do your own research, but don't get affected by the emotional smog of other people's opinions. *Don't believe anything blindly. Trust your instincts and all that you have experienced first hand. Be open and ready to learn more. And remember, you can change your opinions as many times as you like.*

And when we don't know much about a specific topic, we can admit that, too. It is not shameful. We don't need to be an expert on everything. There are plenty of experts out there anyway. You don't need to become one to be happy. Quite in the contrary... I use the word 'expert' in a not so serious way. Why? The more you really know about a particular subject, the less you think you know, and vice versa. The less a person knows about something, the more that person thinks he/she knows... What do you think?

It becomes funny when we pretend to know it all. Because sooner or later, it somehow shows that we really don't! It is much better to say at times:

"I don't know much about this", "I haven't made up my mind," "I don't have an opinion yet."

When communicating with people, let's respect their right to have their opinions. Whether we agree, disagree or somewhat agree is entirely up to us. ***But we all have the right to form our own opinions. The validity of an opinion is yet just another opinion.*** A personal interpretation with a personal meaning.

And when you see things differently you can always ask that person. "Why do you think like that?", "What do you know about it?"

Afterwards, you can present your views based on your knowledge and experience, if you care to.

REALIZATION 43 ~ 45

•

I respect all opinions!

•

I don't need to have too many opinions!

•

I can change my opinions!

•

Sometimes, however, it is better to be quiet. When my feeling tells me that a person simply wants to hear him/herself talk and is not really interested in my views, I shut up. I neither agree nor disagree.

"Aha! Aha!", "I see!" In such a situation I will give my

opinion only when asked specifically.

It is very nice to come across people with whom we can freely exchange opinions and information, where both parties have a desire to learn more. But being in the presence of somebody, who just wants his/her present opinions reinforced is pretty much a waste of time and energy.

The same is true when we talk about personal experiences and end up in an argumentative type of discussion.

"I have done that already five years ago!", "I have been there, too!", "Yeah. I've got the bigger model of that myself!"

Better. Stronger. Smarter. More experienced. Wealthier. The only reason for us to engage in such type of discussions is to get external approval. It is really just another sign of weakness. And whenever we behave in this way, we will just get the opposite anyway. Because nobody likes to hear constantly how great we are.

As we become stronger and more confident within, we don't feel the need to compete anymore. We will automatically avoid arguments. The desire to brag or stand in the limelight all the time is gone for good.

Sometimes it is good to be silently happy, observing a situation, or really listening to a conversation.

Let's agree that senseless arguments are a waste of our time. "I'm too busy to argue with you!", "I don't want to argue with you!", "I have no need to argue!"

It works even when we convey that message quietly, mentally. And yet, we don't need to mind when others do. Just let them. See it for what it is. And let it be.

Sometimes we have to engage in argumentative discussions, especially in the business world. And as long as it is professional, courteous and without emotional smog involved, that's OK. Healthy disagreements can be very constructive.

But often people don't seem to understand what takes place on an energetic level while they argue. Whenever we deny something, it actually reinforces that view. We give it energy by acknowledging that it is something worth spending energy upon. Otherwise we wouldn't feel the need to deny it.

If you don't agree with something or somebody, why waste energy, words and even a thought about it? We can simply dismiss something we believe to be wrong by not acknowledging it, and stating clearly what we think to be true, without first denying what has been said before. Knowing this, we will rarely use the word No anymore.

So if your colleague tells the boss about his/her idea to sell more potato chips and you disagree, don't state your opposition openly and directly. Rather say, that in your assessment, you would go this or that way, for this and that reason.

Let the beauty of your ideas speak for themselves. There is no need to first discard the different viewpoint. Your colleague will surely appreciate your neutrality to his/her proposal. And maybe even come to see that your idea will work better. You make it easier for others to agree with you when you don't trash their ideas and opinions first. In this way you build more consensus and support.

The more often you take a neutral position, seeing things with some distance and from many different angles, the more often your boss and colleagues will ask you about your opinion.

This viewpoint will give you truly the edge, whether it is in your professional or private life. That's the happy way, my friend!

REALIZATION 46~48

•

I can be quiet!

•

I don't need to compete!

•

I don't like to argue!

•

CHAPTER 7

The Big Hurdle

Beware, my friend

Talking about arguments... What often happens when we argue? Yes, we become angry. And who has no experience with getting angry with oneself, with parents or friends, a brother or sister and sometimes with the whole world. Why do we get angry? How can we be less angry?

It is quite obvious that anger kills joy. No matter at whom or what it is directed. Whenever we feel angry in our heart, all joy and happiness is gone. Immediately.

We cannot be happy and angry at the same time as they are complete opposites. Anger causes us to lose vital energy and is always counter-productive. This is true for all anger, justified or not!

In this chapter, we will talk about getting rid of anger and all the associated problems. Once we have mastered this hurdle, we will concentrate on becoming a lot happier again. So, let's see...

Basically, we get angry when we don't get what we want, or somebody behaves differently than we expected.

Whatever it may be that makes us mad, it *always* follows the same pattern. We get emotionally attached first, to something, somebody or particular circumstances. In phase two certain expectations are built up. This is followed by some kind of disappointment. And that's the stage where we become angry.

Some people have a very hard time controlling their anger. They may even lose total control and stop considering potential consequences. Intelligent and rational thinking can become completely blanked out temporarily. That's how strong anger can become.

Frustration and anger accumulate quietly in our subconsciousness over a lifetime. Often we don't even know that it is there. It creates a sense of uneasiness and we may not know why.

Deep inside we know that all the stored anger is not good for our health and well-being. So, we jump at every opportunity to vent this anger.

Some people use their stored anger to deliberately bully others into giving them something, or pushing them into doing what they want them to do. So often we learn this as a child. When we play mad and act furiously, others become intimidated and do what we want.

How do you confront bullies? Well, the best way is to stay relaxed and see such outbursts for what they are: expressions of insecurity, a lack of confidence in one's ability to achieve results otherwise. Then we can politely call the bluff and point out calmly that we are not impressed by such behavior.

"I don't know why you are so angry now. But it doesn't impress me much!", "Why do you become so angry, my friend?", "What does your anger have to do with me?"

If you do know what made a person angry, tell that, too. Often however, we don't and there is no point in speculating. So, we can always ask.

This is a very effective way to distance yourself from other people's anger and diffuse a situation.

We already know what we want and how to get it, and we don't need to push others around to be successful.

REALIZATION 49 ~ 50

•

I can not be intimidated!

•

I don't need to intimidate others!

•

False vs. real calm

Anger is often pushed and shoved around as if somehow that would help us. But redirecting anger at others is not the way to get rid of it. It only builds up more anger as we connect to the anger and negativity of other people. This is true even if we direct anger at people we don't know personally, say, somebody you see on TV.

Anger is an energy vibration with a particular frequency range. It doesn't matter where the anger originally came from, or what caused it.

And as long as we have anger over past, painful experiences and disappointments within ourselves, our anger will start to vibrate stronger when we have contact with another angry person – a person who is actively angry at that moment. Remember the law of induction and resonance?

In the same way, it is like a spark is jumping over from one angry person and activating our own anger potential. That's when we get agitated, too, and start to participate in a war of words, head games, or worse.

Once you have checked out of this vibration range altogether by cleaning up all the anger within, you will still notice anger all around you. But you will not get affected negatively anymore. There is simply no common ground on which to make contact on such a basis any longer.

Angry energy vibrations directed at us will no longer pull us down, but 'fly' through, and return to their point of origin.

Again, when we stay centered and happy, it will have a calming effect on all the people around. You already know how to diffuse tense situations and change them for the better. Point out positive aspects. Change the subject abruptly to a more pleasant one, or crack a joke.

Most people tend to get out of the way when they encounter particularly angry people. It reminds them subconsciously of their own anger. And there is too much potential for trouble present.

But it works the other way, too. The less angry vibes we carry around, the more we will receive invitations to all kinds of parties. People like to be in our company. Because it's more fun and it feels good.

REALIZATION 51 ~ 52

•

I don't want to be angry anymore!

•

I don't need to become angry!

•

Sometimes that is easier said than done. You know what I mean. Let's get into it some more!

One way to be less angry is to become more flexible with our preferences. Instead of having a narrow range of preferences, let's expand them so that we have many more choices available. And there will be always something pleasant to choose from. Imagine that you desperately want to eat ice cream and you drive to town, already looking forward to the cool pleasures to come your way soon. But you only like chocolate ice cream and when you order some, they tell you that they just run out of it. How do you feel? At best you may be disappointed, at worst angry. Where is our happiness gone?

In the first place, we shouldn't become desperate to enjoy something so specific at a specific time. Nevertheless, when we like vanilla, strawberry and banana ice cream, too, we have increased our odds and can probably enjoy some. And if there is no ice cream left at all or the place is closed, we can always enjoy our self in some other ways. ***No more self-imposed limits!***

We can also be less angry when we become more detached. It doesn't mean that we have to renounce the world and move to a monastery, though that may be a way for some people.

Being detached simply means to become mainly attached to being happy. In this way we don't let any disturbances aggravate us and stand in the way of our happiness.

The less expectations we have, the easier life becomes. When we can take things as they come along and enjoy every situation and circumstance to our best ability.

To become detached means also to expect less particular outcomes or results. ***Life is often about improvising. Once we have the confidence that we can always improvise and find a solution to move on, we will stay calm and happy more easily.***

When there is a sudden wall in front of us and blocks the way, we don't need to climb it, swearing and sweating. Instead, let's stay relaxed and *see the easy way.* Keep smiling and just walk around the wall. ***And take the path of the least resistance.*** You can do this even if you are a very ambitious person.

When we don't get what we want and expect, we can just decide to be patient. Knowing that we will get it eventually. It may not be the right time now but the day will come...

Be confident that you can and will realize all your dreams. At the right moment, it will all happen and be. So let's stay happy along the way!

REALIZATION 53~56

•

I don't need to limit my preferences!

•

I am mainly attached to my happiness!

•

I have less expectations!

•

I am patient!

•

To expect less also means to allow the unexpected to happen, that we let go of the urge to control everything around us – and especially, other people. There is always something beyond our direct control.

Trying to control as much as possible is a very stressful way of life. And not a very happy one either. Because there will be always disappointments. They are programmed into such a mindset.

Even very powerful people experience frustration when things turn out differently than they planned or expected.

People are particularly uncontrollable. More often than not, they do the unexpected. And rightfully so. They are in charge of their life and destiny.

We can only choose our way of life. And then live it. That's pretty much a full time job already! It is important to respect the free will of all. As much as we have free will to make our choices in life, so does everybody else.

REALIZATION 57~58

•

I respect the free will of all!

•

I don't need to control others!

•

We can and should always choose to make the best efforts in our life and be happy while we do it, improving things as much as possible, to our best ability.

And accept all that we can not change, what is beyond our control! Say you are at a picnic and suddenly, it starts to rain. Everybody gets soaking wet. Now you can choose. Get mad at the weather or the forecasting service and spoil your good mood, or keep up the spirit and enjoy yourself. You know the song 'Singing in the Rain'? So, just sing and keep smiling! If you catch yourself complaining bitterly, laugh at it and then again, let it be!

The world at large is not yet a perfect place for everybody and all the time. A friend of mine once complained that everywhere he goes and whatever he is doing, money is always involved. People always want and expect money from him, nothing is free, money rules the world. He feels a bit like a walking Dollar sign.

That may be true. But we already know how many of the best things in life are free and how to enjoy them.

Surely, money matters are important, to most of us, anyway. It has been that way throughout history.

So, that's how things are and we can not change it. Instead of feeling aggravated, we can decide to accept it the way it is and live happily, nevertheless, and ever after.

As much as I admire the convictions and drive of political

or environmental activists, I don't see that much happiness present in such circles. Is it really necessary to be angry and frustrated while trying to change the world to the better? Seeing people of different views as enemies to be fought and hated?

To accept the world the way it is now, still leaves the possibilities to contribute somewhere somehow.

Here is the crucial question: will a happy person, being relaxed, a bit detached, with the mental clarity of some distance, produce better results than an angry and complaining person?

Besides, it must be quite tough for somebody who fought for a particular cause all life, being often angry along the way, and come to realize that nothing has really changed. Or not very much anyway.

There is not much joy in such a way of life, and certainly even less gratitude. No matter how well the intentions were.

There are always things that we don't like, but cannot change. So there is no point in getting angry or feeling frustrated about it. Nobody will come to you and say: "Thanks for leading a life of bitterness and frustrations. I know nothing has changed but, thanks for trying anyway!" Not even that!

We can do our bit here and there, as we feel. Letting things evolve slowly. Having faith that all will turn out well at the end of the day. Happy people can make a big difference and yes, they are happy all along the way!

REALIZATION 59

•

I accept the world as it is!

•

Clearing up past anger can be a difficult task in the beginning. The key is to reflect back and see what caused it. Meditation will help us to see more clearly. Go within, ask questions, and listen to the answers.

Past pain, hurt and disappointments may surface. And now, you have the chance to understand. When you truly understand, you are more than halfway there.

Maybe you have already learnt some important lessons. But you don't appreciate yet fully that whatever happened, helped you. Maybe there is still something in store for you to understand.

"Is there anything I should learn now?" We can come to the point where *we appreciate everything that happened in our life.*

The reason we have come thus far in life already is because of all that happened, without exception.

To know and appreciate this as a fact will help us to see our life in a new and wholesome light.

Once we know the causes and understand all the lessons, we can simply decide to let go. Release all the anger because it serves no further purpose. You don't need it anymore and you don't want it anymore either. So why carry it around? Let it go.

REALIZATION 60 ~ 61

•

I know and understand what caused my anger!

•

I decide to release all past anger!

•

The grand game

We all have the experience of feeling guilty at times. Why do we feel guilty? And who has not made the experience of being blamed for something? Or blame somebody else? Why do we do it?

The **guilt-and-blame-game** has become a widely-played game. Throughout history until now. It looks almost like the world has become so used to it, that it has become addictive.

The grand game starts usually in the family. Parents use it in their attempt to educate their children. And the children use it to get something from their parents.

Maybe you grew up with both parents working and therefore they spent only little time with you. When you often complained bitterly, you quickly realized that you can make your parents feel guilty and they will give you more easily what you want. Or your mother may have told you what a stressful, ungrateful or hopeless child you are. That again, you haven't done your homework and that one day you will end up living in the streets, the shame and embarrassment of the family. You may duly feel guilty now and end up studying. Not because you see the benefits of studying, but because you want to restore peace and harmony.

In these and many other ways, we learn from an early age on how to play the strings of the guilt-and-blame-game. And throughout society we can observe its mechanism – at school and later at work, among friends and foes, with our partners in life, in public life and organizations of all kind.

It has become a vicious circle and we need to find a way out of it if we want to be truly happy!

From early childhood onwards, we get trained. If we follow the rules, we get cookies, chocolates, or whatever. And if we don't, we are expected to feel bad and make amendments. We learn that whenever something goes wrong, it must be somebody's fault. So the worst thing we can do, is to confess that we are the culprits because then we are in trouble. So, what is the natural reaction when we get blamed?

Deny it, deny it and again deny it. "Me? No way, I did not do it!", "It is certainly not my fault!", "I did everything right. Somebody must have messed it up!"

We learn to deflect the attention from ourselves to somebody or something else, maybe to the little brother or sister. Later, it may be a spouse, a coworker, a group in society, another nation, race or religion perhaps, or a different club or political party. Lay the blame at somebody's doorsteps. If nobody obvious can be found, let's put the blame on the "mystery man", a mysterious cause or the great unknown default.

In this way we learn that to lie can get us out of trouble, to not getting caught. And if possible, to leave no proof behind. So we cannot get the blame.

We all just want to be innocent because it becomes a lot easier to enjoy our cookies and chocolates. How can we fully enjoy ourselves when we feel guilty about something?

In Switzerland, there is a southerly warm wind blowing over the Alps and creating the optical effect of the mountain ranges looking closer when viewed from the northerly cities. And over time, people somehow got accustomed to use the "Foen" winds as an excuse for headaches, feeling uneasy and nervous, even heart and sleeping problems. Quite a convenient culprit. The wind doesn't talk back after being blamed!

In other countries where the same or similar winds blow through – for example, the Santa Ana winds in California – people just enjoy the warm weather and have, fortunately, not heard about the Swiss people's tough luck!

Whenever we blame someone else for a mistake or a perceived transgression, we are trying to make that person feel guilty. And when we succeed and that person accepts his/her guilt, we have achieved two things: Firstly, we feel ourselves to be more pure and therefore guiltless, and our subconscious mind will allow us to enjoy something, whatever it may be.

But this feeling of cleanliness will only be temporary as long as we have still more guilt buried within. So, we will again have to find someone else to blame for whatever reason we can come up with.

The second achievement is that we can now manipulate the blamed person to do something for us, whatever it may be that we want that person to do for us or give us. Sounds quite familiar, doesn't it?

Of course, the game works only if the blamed party accepts the blame by duly feeling guilty. But mostly the blame is sent right back to its originator and if that is not possible, somebody or something else is quickly found. The big pushing and shoving around of guilt and blame.

Another way to feel guilty is when we blame ourselves. My wife used to always feel guilty after a particularly enjoyable meal. She felt that she ate too much.

"Oh, too many calories!" or "Oh no, I will gain weight!" Then she did a bit of exercising to feel better about it. It never helped much when I pointed out to her that she really has no reason to worry about her weight. And that it's not really important to me.

But it was for her. And it took her quite a while to overcome this feeling of guilt, indoctrinated by the whims of the fashion world.

Think for a moment how often you blame yourself for something that has happened in the past. How many regrets do you still carry around with you?

As a matter of fact, everybody makes mistakes. I don't know of any exceptions. Sometimes we are aware of a mistake and sometimes not. And of course, the mistakes of powerful people have stronger effects than the mistakes of John Smith. Who doesn't make any mistakes?

Blame always involves the past. "You didn't turn off the water tap. Now the whole bathroom is flooded!" How does that comment help to dry the floor?

We can not change an event of the past. And we all feel

smarter in hindsight. So, instead of distributing blame and guilt, we can decide to shift our attention to the positive.

If somebody blames you, stay calm, think and feel about the situation before you react. There is no rush. Our normal and impulsive reaction would be to deny everything. But if we actually made a mistake, why deny it, or blame somebody else and ultimately make matters worse?

In the first moment, during a heated argument, we might think that it is absolutely, positively not our fault whatsoever. And later on when we are calm again, we may recognize how we contributed our share to the quarrel. We may have hurt somebody's feelings or pushed someone in a corner.

It always takes two to tango. *And things are often different than they appear to be at first!* It is far better to be honest and admit something right away. But better late than never.

If, after reflecting on the situation, you know that you have acted correctly, you can calmly make your point. A friendly, understanding and polite response will be more helpful to the other party, and to yourself because it will leave you with a good feeling.

It is important that we are honest and have the courage to take the responsibility for all that we do in our own life, and that includes our mistakes.

Taking responsibility means to acknowledge a mistake. Learning from it. Understanding why something has happened. Make the conscious decision to not repeat this particular mistake. And if necessary and possible, offer to make good.

Usually, when we truly understand why something has happened, we will automatically not repeat a mistake. All we need to do is seeing and understanding all the facets involved.

And to make up for a mistake is quite easy, too. To honestly admit it, is all that is really needed most of the time. "Yeah, that was really a mistake!"

Offer an apology only when you feel truly sorry, and

only if it is really necessary. There are people that are so insecure that we can recognize them by being overly apologetic. Even if they did nothing wrong and something is obviously not their fault, some people will still apologize for it.

Denying an actual mistake will leave us feeling bad about ourselves, whether we are aware of it or not.

There is a sense of honor in admitting a mistake and taking the responsibility. It feels good within because it is right.

REALIZATION 62 ~ 64

•

We all make mistakes!

•

I know when I made a mistake!

•

I can admit my mistakes!

•

When we get blamed, we usually get mad about it. Especially so, if we feel that we are innocent.

To blame ourselves means to be angry at ourselves because we should have acted differently than we did.

And we have to be angry before we can participate in the blame game. Dishing out blame is a way to vent our anger within.

Have you ever driven your car through rush hour traffic and somebody honked at you, or made obscene gestures? And you were not aware of any mistakes on your side, having observed all the traffic rules properly? Well, now you have two choices:

You get angry for being innocently blamed and you swear back at the guy, adding your repertoire of hand signs.

Or you smile relaxed and friendly and lift up your hand as you would to say "Hi!" to a friend.

The first response would leave you with negative emotions such as stress and anger at being blamed unfairly. Because of your own reaction to this situation, your anger potential becomes activated, and even more piles up.

You might have had a nice day and felt relaxed and happy, and the other person might have had a really lousy day and is frustrated for whatever reasons.

So now, that person got temporarily rid of some negative energies and will be a bit more calm. But the chances are high that you will not continue your singing and whistling while driving on!

The second reaction will definitely leave you in your happy mood. No change whatsoever. You don't connect with the driver's feeling of aggression, frustration or stress.

The other person may now feel either more relaxed after your friendly and warm reaction, or alternatively, even madder because he/she could not succeed in aggravating you by passing on some of the bad day. "Thanks but no thanks, my friend!"

Playing the game of guilt and blame always leaves scars in our mind, either consciously or subconsciously. When we get blamed unfairly, anger builds up. And when we often blame somebody, we also build a mental connection to that person's negative energy fields. Since we started the exchange of negativity, we will feel bad about it, again, often unconsciously. It always goes both ways. The more serious the accusation, the more bad energy flows between people.

Politicians are quite often popular targets for blame,

especially in times of economic troubles. Just see what happened after the collapse in the Asian economies. Fingers were quickly pointed to their so-called corrupt leaders, both corporate and government.

Knowing some things about economics and investing, I knew immediately the name of the game. There may be some corruption in Asia, too, but it had very very little to do with what happened, in my assessment anyway. And where exactly in the world does corruption not exist?

Before we dish out blame and accusations, we should always ask ourselves how we would act in that particular position or situation. Do we really know all the facts?

Say, you are a powerful politician and a corporate lobbyist invites you for a round of golf at a luxury resort. When the private jet is sent to pick you up, would you turn it down and take the bus?

Do discussions need to take place in stuffy buildings? Why not have some fun doing a basically boring and often ungrateful job?

There are certainly serious cases of wrong-doing going on, but can we be the judge? Do we have to be? Would we do a better job? If the answer is yes, why are we not running for an office?

To just criticize is very easy. The same is true for playing the grand blame-game. The grand folly.

Just think how long it takes to plan and build a house, versus destroying one. Being constructive and positive requires more courage. And it is a lot more rewarding...

We are not walking through life with rose-colored glasses, refusing to see reality, when we don't want to blame ourselves or other people. We can notice both our mistakes and the mistakes of others. But it is only helpful when we understand and learn.

To truly understand means to be tolerant. Giving ourselves and others the freedom to choose in life, even if that includes making mistakes.

REALIZATION 65 ~ 66

•

I understand and learn from my mistakes.

•

I am tolerant of mistakes – mine and others!

•

To judge is just another facet of the guilt-and-blame-game. Let's see the difference in these statements: "This guy is such an idiot! I can't believe he did this!" vs "I don't agree with his action. I think it was a mistake!" Which way of expressing yourself will still leave you feeling relaxed and happy?

In the first statement we judge the person as a whole and condemn him to be an idiot. How can we make such a tough judgment? Do we really know that person so well and all the circumstances involved? Maybe that person needed to have that particular experience in order to learn an important message. How do we know? Do we see all the angles of all parties in a dispute in a fair, objective and balanced way? Do we see the motives, feelings and thoughts behind an action or behavior? Probably not.

So the happy way is to always think of a person as being innocent. At least until you really know differently. ***Don't rush to conclusions easily because things are not always as they seem to be.*** Sometimes we put motives into other people's head solely because we think in this or that way...

So let's give others some space and the benefit of the doubt. That will then become increasingly how other people see us and relate with us, too...

To call somebody degrading names is an attempt to feel

superior to that person. And we have already seen that this is always a mistake and wrong.

We cannot really be happy when we need to feel superior to anybody else, or when we make somebody else feel bad in order for us to feel good. It is just a temporary illusion. And it implies that we don't feel good about ourselves in the first place...

With the second statement you clearly disapprove of an action but you still respect the person as a human being. And you may try to understand the reasons why this person acted in whatever manner.

When we blame, judge and condemn other people in an aggressive, absolute and abusive manner, we can not be really happy. There is a part in us which feels guilty and bad about it because it is wrong. Furthermore, we become involved with that person on that kind of wave length.

Fully understanding the guilt-and-blame-game can take a bit of time, but it is certainly worth the effort. The will to stop participating comes when we truly understand and feel all its implications on us and others.

We are getting closer when we have the confidence that we can achieve our goals without forcing anybody to do something for us by making them feel guilty. We will know that others will help us freely because they know and understand us, too. They enjoy our presence, appreciate our friendship and all that we give and stand for, including our occasional mistakes...

Know and understand as much as possible. Tolerate and overlook a lot. And improve whatever you can.

REALIZATION 67 ~ 68

•

I do not need to feel guilty!

•

I don't want to blame or judge!

•

Have you ever experienced the presence of a highly critical person who intently observes you? You can almost see the disapproval and criticism written in that person's face. And every time you say something, you always get an instant negative reaction, such as denying what you have just said, correcting you all the time, and being generally argumentative.

"You could have done it earlier!", "You should have done it this way!", "Why didn't you?", "You shouldn't have...", "I don't think so!", "You're wrong".

Now, I guess it would be a silly question to ask whether you felt comfortable in that situation! Nobody likes to be judged or criticized, neither openly nor behind their back. It simply doesn't feel good.

I used to be quite critical, skeptical and sometimes outright cynical. Although I was otherwise quite sociable, I didn't have many real friends and got often criticized myself.

Once I fully understood what I'm writing about now and started to accept people as they are, unconditionally, my world changed completely for the better.

Remember that people who criticize others are often jealous of something, even the very thing they criticized! They want to have this or that, too, or be like this or that, too.

Of course, this may be hidden in the unconscious part of their mind. Another thing would be to criticize somebody else for a weakness that they themselves project to another person. But in reality it bothers them about themselves. Again, this goes on mostly in the subconscious spheres.

Let's recognize such ploys and see them for what they are! And we might even tell such people that we are aware of what is really going on. But mostly, it is better to just choose the company of more pleasant folks!

No matter how hard we try, even with the best intentions in mind, **we should realize that we can not change people in any way. Nor do we have the right to do so.** Even the best of arguments will not convince anybody to change his/her mind unless that person is willing to change. This willingness to improve oneself and allow changes for the better to happen, produces the necessary freedom of mind to be able to actually listen. To learn and understand more. And eventually, to implement some changes.

We can save ourselves a lot of trouble and pain by simply accepting people the way they are. With all their strengths and weaknesses. And without any conditions attached.

Live. And let others live. Think and let others think. Do. And let others do. Be and let be.

Of course, this does not mean that we have to be with unpleasant type of people. Not at all. We have the right to discriminate and choose our company carefully.

Angry, envious, complaining, bullying, condemning, judging, violent and self-pity types are better left alone. And least in one's private life. But remember the reasons why you meet the people you do. Appreciate them for what you can learn. We can learn both from a good or a bad example...

Sometimes we can't just walk away and we have to deal with certain people, whether we like their character and behavior or not. But, we can nevertheless achieve better and happier results by accepting them. No matter what, things will improve a lot that way!

When people feel that they are totally and sincerely accepted, they will feel very comfortable being in our presence. It is a whole new ball game. And our life becomes a lot more pleasant, too!

REALIZATION 69

•

I accept all people the way they are!

•

Past vs. present

How can we accept a person unconditionally after we had some negative, even painful experiences with them? Should we try to forget it all?

Did you notice how often people relate to each other in the past tense? Why do we do that? Is it helpful for our purpose?

Say you have made a particular experience with somebody in the past. And you know that we all have the tendency to make up our mind about people. Now, you may have put that person into a particular category based on what you experienced together. You have made that conclusion some time ago and that is how you still see him/her at present, too, and relate to that person accordingly. How will that affect you?

This is what happens so often, even when we don't know a person at all. Maybe we have met just five minutes ago and yet we feel an urge to come to some kind of conclusion.

We observe a person's style and manners. We want to know their profession and social status, to categorize people. We want to sort them out and put them in nice and neat little boxes, with short and simple labels.

There is just one problem here. These impressions are just snapshots of particular moments in the past. They may not be reality in the present anymore or they are just part of reality.

As much as we can change our style, opinions and habits as we grow up and become smarter, so do the people we know from the past. It is important that we give each other the space and freedom to grow. And recognize that we can change and others do, too.

I have noticed the confusion of people trying to categorize me. That would be quite a tough job as I have a wide variety of interests. Depending on the issue, I could be perceived as a communist, capitalist, liberal, socialist, conservative, environmentalist or libertarian.

We should realize that this is where the world is heading. There is no simple black and white. The modern world has become a lot more complex than in the 'old' days. People's knowledge and interests have increased tremendously over the last one hundred years and individual topics become more important than simple party politics, the politics of "little boxes." People may on some issues be a liberal and on others a conservative, whatever. Ultimately, our political systems will have to reflect these changes in the way they work.

The world is not standing still; everything moves and develops constantly. And so do people.

Parents often relate to their children based on fixed opinions from the past, and vice versa. This becomes especially obvious, when we meet a person whom we haven't met for many years. It is a bit like being in a time warp where we are suddenly sucked back into a far distant past. Time seems to have stopped and we relate to each other as we would have done before.

We may have changed our opinions, lifestyle, etc., completely and yet, we are confronted with an old and completely inaccurate picture of our self. We are not the same person any longer but are still expected to be! This can be quite a frustrating experience, for both sides.

These expectations that we should be, think and behave in the old ways, can generate a subtle and yet very strong pressure to then actually behave in that way. And very often we do so. We may react in certain ways as we would have done when we were a lot younger. It is like being caught and locked up in a mental cage and can be such a drain of energy. And it may take some time to come back to the here and now again and our present energy levels.

Looking back at such an encounter and seeing it in the proper perspective, we may wonder why we behaved in this or that manner. It is like somebody has pushed us into an old behaving pattern, even though we normally wouldn't behave that way anymore.

So, sometimes we have to communicate the fact that we are aware of others relating to pictures out of our past, and not with our current selves. "Your image of me is past and gone. It is not a fact anymore. Look at me now!"

We can state this openly and friendly, or we can silently communicate it in our mind, sending out these thoughts with love. We don't need to be angry because this mistake is quite commonly made. We have probably made that mistake, too.

It can be quite a wake up call and can bring a relationship to a new and much more enjoyable level, instead of abandoning it lightly. Although this we may have to do if we notice that there is no willingness, no flexibility and no hope for a change to a new and improved relationship based on the realities of the present. Then it is time to vote with your feet.

But relationships with family, and especially one's parents should not be easily abandoned. Here it is important for our happiness, that we keep up our communication with an open heart and mind, no matter how hard that may be at times.

We need to come up with some extra patience. It is very much worth it!

We can avoid being locked into the past by seeing ourselves and everybody else as we are now. And always interact in our present set of mind, without letting past memories interfere too much.

Look at old acquaintances with the same open mind as you would when you meet somebody for the first time. Feel their present energy. Get to know how they think and feel now. And react only to this reality. It is a bit like being a tailor who takes new measurements each time a customer shows up. Even regular clients change their body weights and sizes all the time, so a tailor cannot just refer to the old measurements from the last job. The suit would simply not fit properly.

When we relate to people with such an open, free and flexible set of mind, we will make it easier for them to see us more the way we are now, too.

It is a very invigorating and pleasurable experience!

REALIZATION 70

•

I see people as they are now!

•

CHAPTER 8

Getting There

The final approach

We have already covered quite a few hurdles in the way of a happier lifestyle and understand what happens to the subtle energy levels and flows. And yet there is much more ahead of us. In this chapter we will bring all the previously discussed realizations to a successful conclusion. And in the last chapter we will learn to turbocharge it all to ever new heights...

We came to realize that no matter what we do, it will have an influence back on us. Our words, our thoughts, feelings and actions. All that we do, think, feel and say.
Whatever information goes into our mind through our senses will have an effect.

If we don't control our lives and what influences our mind and well-being, we can be sure that somebody else will, or worse, already does, **where choices are made for us, but not necessarily with our best intentions in mind.** Advertising is a good example of trying to win over the minds of people. Yes, it is good to know what products are available to us, but we need to have the will and determination to discriminate between fact and fiction.

We have to separate real product information from the marketing hype which conditions us to behave in certain ways, like buying a particular product or service at a particular time, thus turning us into consuming robots without active thinking or independent decision-making.

During the many years I was involved in the marketing and sales of Swiss luxury watches, I met many advertising executives from around the world. I was often puzzled how frequently our marketing messages were published using the exact words I had written. And I'm not talking about advertising here, but reports in all kinds of publications. It looked like a journalist had written the article, but mostly, our words and messages were used without any critical and independent research into our claims.

A lot of advertising is based on lies or fiction. Not

necessarily in terms of the content, but the way it is presented. I came to that conclusion after seeing how pictures in both print and electronic media are manipulated. TV commercials, for example, often use totally different products to give the desired optical effects. Sales pitches of various kinds appeal to our different emotions. It is quite amazing to see what kind of money is spent on a multitude of advertising efforts. And obviously, nobody would spend such amounts without knowing that it will come back many times over.

If you don't control your mind, somebody else will. Think about that.

Once we are fully aware of this fact, we become increasingly more selective of our choices and distinguish between happy and unhappy influences. And start to reject all that influences us in a negative way, focusing instead on positive and uplifting choices.

So next time you will hear the Rolling Stones singing, "I can't get no satisfaction!", think twice before you start to sing along. It is amazing how often nice music is accompanied by depressing or sad messages.

See and hear it for yourself!

Television is emanating not just electromagnetic waves but lots of emotional energies. It is a visual medium that directly affects our brain through the eyes. There is less active involvement for the mind than while reading a book or newspaper.

TV shows and movies can send us on an enormous emotional rollercoaster ride. While watching a movie, who is in charge of your emotions? You or the film's director? It's your choice. If you are aware of it...

Stay in charge of your destiny at all times. I still watch and enjoy movies, but I'm aware of what is happening. And I decide to what extent I let it influence me. And I learned to discriminate everything that influences me...

Do you know what I would recommend to a very depressed person as an immediate first aid treatment?

Switch off the TV and radio for two weeks. No newspapers, either. If your job requires you to know the latest news, read just those specific news items. Scan the paper or the net quickly for the headlines. When you are focused, you will just see what you need to see.

That's it. Very simple and yet, very effective. Guaranteed! We can all survive with less news. Or even no news for a few weeks. You don't need to take in the latest body count twice a day to know what is happening in the world.

We will can still notice undesirable energies and yet, remain unaffected. The less we expose ourselves to activities and environments draining us of energy, the stronger we become.

Concentration on everything that we like and love is a key ingredient in the total recipe leading us to a happier life!

As our sensitivity to the energies around us expands further, we become accustomed to reading energy.

We can read or feel the energy of a situation, a particular environment, people and objects, or the energies of cities, states and entire countries.

You can do the energy test even with food. See whether it has a strengthening or weakening effect, before we eat it. By holding it, looking at it, feeling it!

We are able to scan and feel the whole spectrum of energies, from the lowest to the highest of frequencies. We can distinguish between what feels good and what doesn't. We have a strong inner knowing of what is uplifting to our spirits and what is not, what makes us happy and what doesn't.

You know that whenever you feel really happy, you feel also strong and confident. You have no fears and worries. You feel full of vital energy, healthy and on the top of the world. ***So, high energy literally translates into happiness. A happy person's energies vibrate automatically on a higher level and in a harmonious and balanced way.***

And whenever we feel down, being consumed by negative emotions and interactions, our energy level is lower than normal.

Our normal state of being is naturally full of harmony and joy. When we vibrate on lower energy levels, we are out of balance with the natural state of our being, indeed, with the natural order of the universe.

So, the first steps we took together, was to eliminate the reasons for conflicts and the according drainage of energy. Then by checking out of lower or negative vibration levels, we reached the point of not getting affected by such energies any longer, neither actively nor passively.

This is a bit like being in a neutral state where we feel again more centered within ourselves. The natural strength of our innermost being can start to again express itself because it is no longer weakened. The sun starts to dissipate all the clouds until there is only sunshine left. And now, only the sky will be the limits...

Perfect health

We have looked at health issues already in the bigger concept of different energies. Now is the time to make some final conclusions to stay healthy, or become healthy. We don't need to look at specific diseases, just what causes them, primarily...

You know that our bodies are influenced on the more gross energy levels by what we eat and drink, how well we sleep and whether we do some exercising or not.

Here are the only important keywords to remember: ***Moderation, moderation, moderation.*** Anything that we carry to extremes will have a negative reaction of some sorts.

Find a well-balanced, middle way to all forms of extremes and you will be in good health. It is as simple as that.

Everything can become poisonous if we overdo it. This is true of foods and drinks, exercise and sleep. Too much of it is not beneficial for our health and neither is too little. *A healthy balance is also a happy balance!*

But even if we indulge ourselves occasionally in extremes or have some unhealthy habits, we should certainly not feel guilty about it. Or worry about it. Because here we enter again the enormous influence sphere of our mind, where we can either neutralize negative physical effects to a large degree, or alternatively, make them a lot worse.

Substance abuse is something very natural. It has been going on for thousands of years. We abuse legal or illegal drugs for different reasons.

It may be a hidden death wish which leads to self-destructive behavior, or it is simply the desire to change the present reality. We may want to experience new worlds and realities in our search for perfect happiness and bliss.

Whatever the reasons may be, we all like to use and abuse things. That is a simple fact. Some people get addicted to sex, chocolates, alcohol, sleeping, jogging, working, watching TV. You name it.

Addictions seem to be more the norm than the exception. No matter what it may be for you, don't feel guilty about it. Ever.

Let's take smoking tobacco as an example. But before we do, I wish to add the little disclaimer here that I own no tobacco company's shares or have any other incentive from such companies whatsoever. Also, this is not meant to encourage you to smoke. Not at all. We all know that it is not the smartest thing to do. Every smoker knows that, too.

Mankind has used tobacco in various ways over thousands of years as a stimulant and form of enjoyment. There are people in remote areas of Asia, such as Myanmar, Laos, etc., who have rolled and smoked cigarettes all their life and they are over a hundred years old. They live otherwise a rather relaxed, natural and healthy lifestyle in the midst of their extended families, without much stress and worries.

But if you do the same, living in a hectic city, not eating balanced food or exercising enough, and are rushing daily through your professional and private life, chances are that smoking will become a life-shortening affair.

There are many examples of people who smoked and reached over a hundred years old. They have balanced their bad habits by otherwise sound and healthy habits. And then, there are people living in big cities that have never smoked and died of lung cancer anyway.

So many things can become harmful to somebody's

health. Stress, pollution, worries and fears are just some of the factors. If we want to become sick and pass away, there are literally thousands of possibilities to do so.

It is not just a matter of your genes, luck, coincidence, or the like. How we live and die depends on our overall being, our personality, our thinking, our feelings and way of life.

There may be all kinds of potential diseases stored in our gene pool but that doesn't mean that any of them will actually need to break out. These are just potential possibilities and not at all a certainty as every serious doctor can confirm. The question here is: Let's say you know that there is a certain sickness potentially latent among your gene pool and you often worry about developing this sickness. Is there now a bigger chance of you actually getting it than if you don't worry about it?

There are billions of microbes, bacteria and viruses in the air we breath. Most bacteria are beneficial to our health and our bodies are full of them. They perform certain functions, especially in the intestines. And surely, some small percentage of the total could bring about some diseases. But it doesn't mean that we will develop them.

When we are strong and happy, vibrating at high energy levels, our immune system works properly and all is fine. Potentially there are many ways we could become sick. The emphasis here is on *potentially!* It doesn't need to be.

It is a bit funny to see how people sometimes show their fears of disease. Just look around in a closed room during the winter months and see the reactions of people when somebody is sneezing or coughing out loudly. Terrified looks and faces all around, sometimes annoyed or even angry.

In a way it's not really funny, but a bit sad. When you worry about catching the flu, do you actually increase your chances of getting it or not? Try it out. In my experience yes, it certainly does!

Coming back to smoking, we can see that nowadays, every packet carries doomsday messages. "Smoking kills" and the like. It doesn't say that it may shorten your life but says that most definitely and absolutely, with all the authority of the government, that it does kill. Of course, these governments have the best of intentions and prefer people to be healthy, rather than increasing the costs of the public health systems any further. And they certainly don't want to be sued for taking taxes on these products. But are such messages smart when we consider that some people will actually believe it and duly die? Maybe sooner than they otherwise would have? We have already seen the effects of words and these carry additionally the psychological weight of the government's authority.

Australian tobacco products carry certainly the largest and visually most shocking messages. And it scares a lot of people. I heard of shopkeeper's accounts of how some customers react. Often, people tell me how frightened they are.

All this reminds me of the prognosis of some doctors who may think that they know best. I know several people who were diagnosed with severe diseases and were given just a couple of months to live and clean up their worldly affairs. Two believed them and duly passed away. And two friends very dear to me, didn't, and lived another thirty years...

Some people just believe such dire predictions too easily and think of their doctor as being a superhuman authority to be trusted literally with their lives, and give up their hopes and efforts to overcome their situation.

So if you have a bad habit, stay cool, be happy, and don't feel guilty, bad or ashamed about it. This would be really bad for your health. Try to reduce, say the amount of cigarettes you smoke a day, believe in yourself, the healing powers within yourself and concentrate on becoming more and more happy. And as you do and increase your energies, you will find that one day you can easily just stop and quit.

When you don't need it anymore, it will just fade away from your life. For good.

Invoking fears or stirring up already existing fears are great selling tools for some companies, political parties, governments and all kinds of religions. Don't get caught in such games.

In Australia, they started a dire advertising campaign to

sell mobile telephones to women. They did it in such a scary way as if women were risking their lives without having one!

Or look at the marketing campaign for sunscreen lotions showing cute baby pictures and severe warnings, as if mothers would take their babies out to the beach and let them fry there the whole day long!

Part of the year I live in the tropical part of Australia, the most beautiful place I have seen anywhere. Even though the sun is strong, I normally don't use sunscreen lotions. Why?

Because the sun feels good on my skin and I like it. But during the hottest time, between 10 am and 4pm, I don't spend much time outside.

When you read the energy of the sunshine and it feels good, it will be good. So don't worry!

The suns rays are very invigorating, can heal or maintain good health. White light consists of all the spectrum of colors. Colors are energetic wave lengths and are successfully used in color therapies for healing.

In July 1999, a team of respected academics in England published their conclusion that sunbathing is beneficial to our health. It increases happiness among all the other benefits. Surprise, surprise?

During all these years, when dire campaigns were scaring people out of the sun, depression was steadily on the increase. Coincidence? Perhaps.

Of course, if we overdo sunbathing, as with everything, it becomes harmful. But being sensitive, we will feel when it is time to get out of the sun or put on a sunscreen.

To slap on creams all the time which also filter out parts of the light spectrum, and being fearful and worried while enjoying the sun, is really not necessary. But fear sells...

There have been so many studies and campaigns in the last thirty years, trying to tell us how and what to eat. And a decade or so later the old dogmas were discarded. New evidence was coming out, sharply contradicting all the previously held beliefs.

To follow the latest recommendations is quite difficult these days. And even as a former health fanatic, I came to the point where I'm not interested to know the latest dogmas. I used to live as a very strict vegetarian for more than ten years and continued to learn about the latest on wholesome foods. Was I healthier than now? No, quite in the contrary. My mind was still full of worries and fears. Now, I do as I please. I listen within and I know what to do, what to eat, and so on. Very simple.

So, stay cool and happy. Don't worry about what might happen and you will live a lot healthier. Being afraid does not make your life any better, just more miserable.

If you are a fearful person, write down your fears on a piece of paper. All of them. Get them out of the system. Look at how many of them are totally unnecessary. Often they are not even your own, but learnt fears projected by parents, friends or society at large.

Remember the time when you were a kid and how fearless you were then. Until you were told that this and that is terribly dangerous. And suddenly, you started to believe it and stopped doing what you basically enjoy doing!

Some say that fears are essential instincts for our survival. This may be true if it makes us go through life with open eyes and being careful in certain circumstances. Being mindful of potential dangers is OK, but a lot different from being afraid!

Confronting our images of fear can be quite a challenge, but it is good to do it. I was afraid of heights, not as a child, but later on. So I decided to learn to fly little airplanes and confront this fear. Becoming a pilot is not all that difficult by itself. But overcoming these fears, especially when practicing stalls, spins and the like, was quite tough for me.

At one stage I was terribly afraid of sharks to the extent that I didn't feel like swimming in the ocean. That was probably after seeing the great white shark movies! So I took up diving. I thought that if I went underwater to see for myself what is there, it would help me to overcome this fear. It did. So, look your fear into the eyes, and it will blink – an old saying, but true nevertheless.

Another aspect about fears is their tendency to become true. The more we are afraid of something and keep on worrying about it, the more we actually attract such events into our lives.

So, unless we have come the point where we are fearless and can truly laugh about it, I would suggest that often watching horror movies, psycho thrillers etc., is not a very good idea.

Fortunately, at night, our mind is "reset" and not all that we put into our minds, need to become a reality. We may end up with a nightmare, nevertheless. ***It all really depends on how often we do, think or say something. And it also depends on the intensity, clarity, and strength of our thoughts!***

The more frequently and intensely you focus on a thought or a dream, the quicker this thought or dream manifests itself in your reality.

Meditation is an excellent way to reset our mind and to let go of all our fears.

In the end, all fears are related to death, where we fear that we may cease to exist. To really overcome this fear is only possible when we become spiritually aware. And we will talk about it soon.

For now, let's see that fears are a source of unhappiness, a source of sickness and even exploitation. And therefore, we don't want them, we don't need them, they are completely unnecessary!

REALIZATION 71 ~ 72

•

I don't want to be afraid!

•

I do not need to be afraid!

•

People can develop symptoms of sickness just by feeling lonely and depressed. Or when they feel that they are not being accepted and loved. In the USA alone treatments of imagined sicknesses are estimated to cost about twenty billion dollars per year. And this is probably just the tip of the iceberg when we consider how many real diseases are being caused by disharmonies originating in the mind.

Sickness is a cry for help, a cry for love. When a loved one is sick, you don't necessarily help by acknowledging the disease and say: "Oh, poor darling, I feel so sorry for you"! Because that may be the whole intention after all, knowingly or unknowingly.

And by acknowledging a disease and offering pity, we reinforce it by adding more energy and thus actually make it more real, stronger, and more severe.

There is a delicate middle way we have to find between acknowledging and ignoring. Complete ignoring will make the patient angry at us, and that's not good for anybody. But rather, since we know that a sick person wants more love and attention, we can give just that. There are more or less subtle ways to do that and it depends on your relationship and that person's character. But see for yourself how well it works!

A couple of years ago I read about a couple who raised their kids to become healthy and strong adults in this unusual way: At a quite early age, whenever the kids became sick, the parents just put all the tools and medicine in their room and told them to stay in the room until they get well. They were neither allowed to watch TV nor play. No fun whatsoever. It was almost a kind of punishment. And strangely, the kids grew up and forgot about becoming sick, they don't get even the flu anymore. They just saw that there was no point in becoming sick. It was no fun and served no purpose!

Another reason why people become sick is more subtle and not so widely understood yet. We looked at the guilt-and-blame-game quite in detail and already saw the negative energy exchanges and accumulation taking place.

Yes, guilt is a major reason for sicknesses and other forms of suffering. Feelings of guilt within our minds are very powerful even if we suppress them to the subconscious area where we "think" that some form of suffering can right some past wrongs. Of course, it works that way mostly without us being aware of it.

Our subconscious mind sends out energies and attract some forms of suffering into our lives. It can be just a minor sickness or discomfort. But it may also be something more severe.

Feelings of guilt cause people to think that they should not be happy, that in fact they don't deserve to be happy! This is very unfortunate because it is entirely unnecessary. There is no real reason why we need to become sick and suffer, or become victims.

We can learn about our mistakes and its lessons without it. ***When we want to learn and improve our lives, striving to be perfectly happy, we can transcend the need for all misery.***

Any form of suffering will not change a past event. It is as simple as that. Punishment has no meaning unless we learn what we need to learn. Doing so voluntarily and with joy is the better option.

Yes, there are still people who break the most basic rules necessary for the harmonious functioning of society. Stealing and aggression in any form are obviously very serious mistakes and yet they still happen. But no punishment reverses what happened already. In my view, there are possibilities where such people can learn how wrong their mistakes have been. Where they really understand and feel truly sorry. Being truly sorry normally means that they will not cause another person to suffer again.

Just locking people up and throwing away the key will not do that. Neither do cries for revenge. Because violence brings only more violence. Besides, there are always cases where such justice is applied to innocent people. In my opinion, violence is only justified as a last resort of self-defense.

Those who have transformed themselves can be reintegrated into society. There are various ways to do that and in the next chapter we will look at an easy and effective way to actually help others without getting negatively affected.

And if there are people where any help doesn't bring about a real change in understanding and behavior, then they should be banished. Like in some native societies of the older days. People who could not fit in a peaceful, non-violent society had to leave the clan. They were not allowed to ever return.

There could be some very large sections of uninhabited areas fenced off, with surrounding mine fields and observed electronically by satellites. They would be forced back to nature without any outside help like food, clothing and shelter. To survive in the natural habitat would be quite a full time job.

They would be free to move around and do anything they please. We would just recognize that people who behave like barbarians and savages are not yet civilized and therefore have no place in our civilization.

If a person has a real predatory state of mind, that person poses always a danger to peaceful members of society. **You can respect and even love a lion but knowing of its predatory character, you wouldn't choose to hang around with one. Or hug one.**

We can respect such people as people, no matter what they did, and give them their space to live where they can look after themselves. Nature can be harsh but is a very good and fair teacher. It would give those people the chance to make some progress at their own leisure. To live freely in nature, literally back to the roots, doesn't need to mean suffering. But it means living without the modern comforts of civilized societies. This would, in my view, be a more generous and civil approach than the call for revenge.

Revenge is not a necessary way of thinking for everybody. The above solution would certainly have a scaring-off effect on those concerned, in its own subtle ways.

Sometimes I see people on TV all aggravated and shouting for revenge, crying for blood. They don't seem to know what they are doing. They actually connect themselves to the lower energies of the person whose head they are calling for. Not a very happy and pleasant exchange at all.

This little excursion was to show that there are really no people whom we should hate or condemn to suffering, if we want to be happy.

Even when we store justified anger, it will still have the same negative effects on our health, well-being and happiness. It is like a car that is quietly but steadily rusting from the inside out...

And it is not at all necessary when we understand that sooner or later the chickens come always home to roost!

Everybody sets up their own destiny, anyway. All actions will bring about a reaction.

Most people who feel guilty, condemn themselves for just minor mistakes and transgressions. If we don't need to hate and condemn people who make the most severe of mistakes, then there is really no reason to condemn ourselves for our small mistakes in life.

To be tolerant, generous and forgiving with one's self and others is equivalent to passing an important milestone on the road to happiness.

So let's forgive ourselves and others.

Truly forgiving means to understand and then forget. Apologies are not even needed anymore.

When we can finally just letting it go and be. Knowing, that we all deserve to be happy, and healthy, and wealthy.

REALIZATION 73 ~ 76

•

I don't need to be sick!

•

I don't need to suffer to learn!

•

I forgive because I understand and forget!

•

I deserve to be happy, healthy and wealthy!

•

Perfect wealth

Talking about wealthy. Surely you are curious now how to become wealthy. We had some preliminary discussions about it already. And yes, it is time to talk seriously about money. Let's see to it that we always have plenty of it!

We looked at how our mind works in filtering all the input coming through our senses. How it constantly gives us conscious or subconscious feed backs.

Our mind set sends out signals to the external world and interacts constantly. Or put differently, **where the mind goes, the energies will follow.** The energy waves sent out, search for the preferred set of choices and send back similar energies. This is what we then we notice and accept as reality.

So our mind works a bit like a radio station. It transmits programs on particular frequencies and receives simultaneously the corresponding programs we are tuned into. *And we have seen that we can change the way our mind thinks as we change software programs in computers. The hardware and basic principles of how it works stay the same. But different mind sets produce different input and output.*

Now we can apply this knowledge too in creating a new reality for us where we have always abundant wealth at our disposal. Where we no longer need to worry about money matters.

But first, let's briefly look at a major obstacle in achieving material success. Who has never experienced being envious or jealous in some ways? Or noticing other people being envious at some of our achievements?

Envy is a primetime success buster. *People that easily become envious of the success, wealth, and fame of others create a situation which guarantees that they will stay in their present situation.* And they will not achieve what they really desire in their hearts.

Envy blocks the good fortunes from flowing in. To be envious means to acknowledge that we are not content with our present circumstances. It is a form of complaining and feeling bitter about perceived injustices. "How come this guy gets all the goodies? I should at least have it, too, because I'm such a nice guy. Why not me?"

Some people are also envious when they see someone else being happy and enjoying their life. And this kind of envy can also come from family members and supposedly loved ones. Even when the happy person is not rich at all, it can still be bothering them. In the presence of such people it is better to be quietly happy, if you have to stay around.

To think in such a manner creates negative emotions and energies. And our positive and higher energies become covered up and have no chance to express themselves. It is not a happy situation to be in.

We can redirect such a mind set when we choose to see successful people, who already enjoy what we want to enjoy too, as role models. Not necessarily in all aspects, but the ones we desire. See success as a motivating force which helps us to bring about constructive changes to the better, too.

People who have achieved success are the living proof that it is also possible for us to come to that point in our life. Right?

Your dreams can become true, too, if you really want them to... Imagine the power of your mind. It is faster than anything else. Mind speed is so much faster than even the speed of light. Just think of a place you visited on your last vacation, and immediately you are there already! That's how fast it is.

There is no reason why your dreams shouldn't become a reality. Temporary obstacles or difficulties are certainly no reason as there are so many successful people who have made it to fame and fortune, literally coming from scratch. Very often they started out with nothing at all and were living in bleak and desolate circumstances.

It can be quite inspiring to read the memoirs of such people. And as we have seen before, big obstacles, problems and suffering are truly not necessary either...

Remember to keep things simple and there will be less complications and problems. Simple solutions are always elegant, easy and quick to implement. But some seem to think: "Why make it easy if you can make it complicated?"

This is certainly not the happy approach to life. Recognize that all problems are really 'homemade'. There is no need for that.

Once we have fully realized this as a fact, we will move along our life a lot more gently and a lot happier!

So next time you see somebody driving up in front of the restaurant in the Rolls Royce that you fancy, be happy. Enjoy the view of the beautiful car and feel happy for the proud owner, too.

You can even wave the guy a friendly hello and smile. And if he comes to your table and asks if you know each other, you can simply say: "Not yet, I was just happy to see you driving along in my favorite car. My compliments!"

It could be the beginning of a nice friendship. Or some exciting opportunities.

At the least, you have enjoyed a nice view and are happy anyway. With yourself, the nice food and your happy company.

The road to riches starts by being content with your life and all that you have at present. Appreciate what you already have at your disposal. Feel content and rich even though you may have more desires, unfilled as of yet.

Being rich is relative anyway. Most people with regular incomes who travel to a poor country are regarded as super-rich there and their present savings would support a lavish lifestyle in the impoverished country.

Surround yourself with beautiful possessions. Not necessarily the most expensive goods carrying famous designer brands. But have some of those too if you can afford it.

Have maybe less goods than you desire, but always strive for the best quality. *Go for quality rather than quantity.* Participate in a flea market and sell all the old junk that you accumulated over the years. Some people will love it and pay you good money for it.

I have done it and it felt just great! Get rid of everything that makes you feel miserable. *Buy and keep only what you really need and like. Treasure those belongings, look after them well and enjoy them.* Enjoy the craftsmanship; its superior functions, quality and design. Truly appreciate all that, feel blessed and be a happy owner. *In this way you will feel already rich.*

This mind set sends out the right signals to all the atoms making up the universe. You will attract just beautiful objects which you treasure and feel good about.

Know always how much money you have and keep all money matters neat, tidy, and honest. Feel good about this money, even if you desire more. And who doesn't?

Don't feel bad about money or guilty about having money in any way. *See it as an enjoyable and pleasurable form of energy.* Because that's what it is! Energy. And we can attract unlimited energy.

As we get happier, we also become stronger. We get used

to operating on increasingly higher energy levels.

And as we are also more confident of ourselves and life in general, we can look at money in this new way:

The energy which we deserve and which allows us to buy all the goods and services we desire.

Money becomes a means to experience life. It is a bit like having a set of tools in the house. No big deal.

We consider a tool kit to be a useful thing to have, but we wouldn't lose much sleep over it, when we don't have it either.

So, now we can see money in a more neutral way, without anxieties and worries attached to it.

Having enough money no longer becomes a life or death issue. In most parts of the world people don't starve to death anymore. There are still a few places where people are hungry and die of malnutrition, and hopefully, this will stop soon. There are political and environmental factors involved which may be difficult, but can be overcome with time. And with individual and mutual effort.

Chances are that since you could afford this book, or could get it in a library, you don't live in such an unfortunate place. In western countries even homeless people don't die from hunger.

Money doesn't need to symbolize security when we feel strong and secure within. And it certainly doesn't need to stand for status and power as this will not increase our happiness anyway. It is quite a mistake to feel more important than others just because we have more money at our disposal.

So let's have all the money we want and need. Let's enjoy the freedom money brings. And let's share some of our extra money with our fellow friends on planet Earth!

REALIZATION 77 ~ 80

•

I am motivated by signs of success!

•

I am content with all aspects of my life!

•

Money is energy and available to me in all abundance!

•

I feel rich and wealthy!

•

Have you ever given some flowers, chocolate or a fine bottle of wine to your dinner hosts or friends and heard an embarrassed, "Oh, you shouldn't. That was really not necessary!"?

What kind of message does this send out to the universe? It says that presents and gifts, which are free, are not welcome. Do you think that such a person sets him/herself up for an abundant lifestyle?

Accept presents and all that is given to you with grace, joy and appreciation. Regard it as a blessing by the universe.

In this way we should also accept invitations and not refuse them lightly. We get invited to a free meal or a boating trip for a reason. Even if you don't like boats very much, go along and enjoy yourself.

You never know what other positive surprises will come from this. Maybe another guest will turn out to be the rich "Prince Charming", you fall in love, and he now wants to marry you!

These are all free forms of energy coming into our lives and we should train our mind to that concept. ***Accept it. Energy is free.*** We can receive unlimited energy in our meditations, for example. It is not that somebody suddenly says: "Stop right here, go away, you had enough already!".

There is no partial authority out there to withhold the energies of the universe to any of its children. ***Money is just another form of this same energy. There is plenty of money and goods in the world.*** It is just not equally distributed. Some people have more because they receive or grab more. But there is no reason why this flow of money should not come into your direction, too.

Let it happen. Pull it in, let it flow in, see it coming your way. Feel rich and you are open and ready to accept more wealth.

Once I was meditating, feeling the endless energies flowing in and I saw that it might just as well materialize as money in my life. Why not?

I felt strong and was totally convinced that this was a fact. And the same day it turned out to be so! I decided to put this reality to the test and did the (for me) unusual thing of buying a lottery ticket. And yes, I won.

OK, it was not the multi-million dollar jackpot, but about eight hundred dollars. Yet I accepted it, nevertheless, with appreciation and joy.

When the shopkeeper told me that I won, she almost couldn't believe it, and repeated it several times. She and others in the store looked quite puzzled that, although I was happy and smiling, I didn't seem to be very surprised. That's because I wasn't.

Don't expect to be rich if you don't love this form of energy. Money. There is nothing wrong, dirty or 'unholy' about it.

Some people seem to think bad about money and even talk bad about money. "Wash your hands, you just touched money. Money is dirty, so many people have touched it!"

But people touch many other things in public places and then go and grab a couple of pizza slices. And a very very small percentage drop dead from that. Others say that they cannot handle money and are then surprised not to have any. Or not much anyway.

At the very least we should have a neutral attitude to money, rather than a negative one.

"Money corrupts! It brings out the worst in people!" That may be true for some people, but that's what they chose to do, or be. It has nothing to do with me. Power corrupts some people too, but not everybody! ***Money just is.*** What each person makes with it, is nothing but a personal choice.

Money does a lot of good. If you don't believe me, become a sponsor to a foster child in Africa and see what kind of letters you will receive!

When saying that we should love money, then of course, it doesn't mean that we should adore or glorify it, making its pursuit the only goal in life. Certainly not. Just see it for what it is.

A form of the great universe's energy and as such it is lovable. And it is open to all of us without limits. This is the attitude to make us rich.

Now, if you are really convinced that this is so, and it is, then you might just as well get all the money you ever need by attracting a multimillion dollar jackpot into your life instead of working hard and struggle.

But even if you are not fully convinced of this and think that you cannot see and handle all the energies on different levels perfectly yet, it will still work. You may have to make an effort some way or another to increasingly receive more money instead of just snoozing off!

But realizing all the above will help you along your way to more riches. There is no need to fight hard for our survival, although some people seem to think so.

Just consider the concept of free energy. Feel it. See it, everywhere you look. In nature for example, birds just fly around, sing and play. And when they are hungry, they look for some food and just take it. No big deal.

REALIZATION 81~83

•

All energy including money is free!

•

I love and accept free money!

•

I am rich!

•

Now, I'm not suggesting that you just go out to a bank and grab some money. That is not a lasting way to keep the money and it is certainly not the way to a relaxed, harmonious and happy lifestyle. But trust yourself, your abilities and most importantly of all, know and feel your connection to All That Is. **We all deserve to be rich and happy! We know now that our mind has power and that we pull all persons and things into our lives.** The stronger and more focused our mind becomes, the quicker we can see the results of this process.

Whether we concentrate on our happiness, our health or wealth... Ultimately, it could all become true at mind speed... The ***calmer*** our mind becomes the sharper and stronger it will be...

We already know how to filter out all the unnecessary and unwelcome noises and disturbances. And now, we can make it happen. We can achieve all that we desire.

In the beginning, the cluttered mind is not really able to see this as a reality. In this state, we send out a lot of conflicting signals to the universe and we are not always happy with the results. But as we get stronger, we will recognize that the timelag between our strongly expressed desires and its fulfillment becomes shorter and shorter.

So here we should be extra careful and express ourselves very precisely. Otherwise we might get results that we don't really want to get.

We have to be sure what we really want, sure about what makes us happy. Even think about the consequences of our wishes. See a situation before it is an actual fact and feel whether we would feel comfortable with it. And if you are, concentrate strongly on this desire, state calmly and with clear awareness your wish and then, **see yourself already in the final picture!** Don't just see the red Ferrari, but see yourself driving it and enjoying yourself!

Now let me suggest that you take out your list of dreams and desires again. Your Plan. Now, go ahead! You know how to do it!

REALIZATION 84

•

I get all that I want!

•

CHAPTER 9

Love Affairs

Definitions

Here we go to the final round. And I have saved the best part for last, where everything we have discussed can be become reality a lot faster – the turbo-charger of it all.

We have covered quite a bit of territory together. Our mind got calmer and clearer and stronger. Now we are in control of our mind. We are no longer being dragged around by external influences where we could just react. And we are out of the emotional swamps. For good.

We control our mind through our willpower, and our mind can create new realities as we 'will', as we want, as we direct it.

You know now that your will can make your dreams come true if you really want them to.

Now the next question is: Who are we? Who directs the mind through this willpower? Who 'wills'?

We already came to the conclusion that we exist simultaneously in different dimensions at the same time. Our body is part of ourselves and so is the mind.

But obviously as we got better and better in directing our mind, we know that we must also be something else. We have to exist again on another level otherwise this wouldn't be possible. In other words, we are not just our minds. In the same way as we are not just bodies!

Here we enter the world of spirit. It is not a logical world in the sense that we can make absolute statements or argue about it. It is very much a world of personal experience. With spiritual awareness it becomes a lot easier to be happy, healthy, strong, wealthy and wise. We enter the **world of love** rather than emotions and we will look at some pitfalls on the way, too.

We have talked about love before. We defined it as a **real feeling**, as opposed to emotions.

Some people may be attracted to somebody and call it love. This word is used quite lightly these days, but in the truest sense of the word it is rather being abused, at least in my definition and understanding of the word.

Often, "love" is used to describe a physical attraction to mostly members of the opposite sex. We even use the word to say that we really like something very much, say, chocolates or whatever.

Love is often tainted by emotions. Imagine a source of pure water somewhere in the mountains. As the water of the little stream flows further and further towards the ocean, joining others to become an ever wider river, it becomes more and more polluted. In the end it is still water but it doesn't taste the same anymore. It may have become even poisonous to health, or rather, in the context of this book, to our happiness. So it may be better to stay away. Not geographically, but rather by being in that neutral state of mind. It is better than drinking polluted water.

Polluted 'love' is not real love and doesn't have the same beneficial effects. **Real love is always pure, refreshing, and real.**

Love comes in different flavors. Or put differently, it can express itself in five ways and all have their own pleasurable taste: Love between brothers and sisters. Love between friends. Love as a parent. Love as a child. Love between partners.

Most people experience at least a few of these loving relationships. More or less intense, more or less pure.

There are always two sides to love – *active and passive.* We love to love somebody. And we love to be loved by somebody.

Happiness is a real feeling too. It is a description of our natural state of being. Happy is what we automatically are when we have overcome the traps of emotions and the other obstacles previously discussed. **Happiness is our birthright. It is what we want for ourselves when we feel love for ourselves. And it is what we want for all the people we truly love.**

Real love is not something we fall into and can again fall out. Love just is. Always.

Once you truly love somebody you can't just stop it because that person doesn't behave the way you want. That is not love. It is attraction or attachment at best. It is based on conditions.

A mother who truly loves her child, always does. She can't stop it even if she wants to, even if the child grows up to become a criminal! Such a pure love describes love as it is. **Unconditional.** She wants/wills only the best, only happiness for her child. Nobody is allowed to harm the child in any way because pure love doesn't want to see any suffering.

My mate

Most of us look for a partner with whom we can share our life with. A person we can love and who loves us back. A person we can come to understand and who understands us. A person we can trust and who can put his/her trust back into us. A person who supports us and we can give support. Somebody with whom we are happy being with.

This is a very natural drive we all share. Everybody wants to love and be loved, at least by somebody. We all seek love automatically, it is an integral characteristic of our innermost being. It is not something we learn later in school but it is a built-in feature in every baby already.

Later in life when we look for a partner, we may become attracted to somebody. And we 'fall in love'. Sometimes we get 'burned out' when we get rejected or endure other unpleasant, even painful experiences. So some people learn to be careful when it comes to love matters. They don't easily trust other men or women anymore.

It doesn't need to be that way when we learn to distinguish between attraction, attachment and love.

It usually goes in this order. The first attraction is often just a physical attraction. And it may grow into real attachment and finally love. But that is not something we can expect to be automatically so. It depends on us, our feelings, thoughts and actions. And those of our partner.

When choosing our partner for life, or our 'soul mate', we should be honest with ourselves and the person we meet. See whether we "click" on the physical, mental, and ultimately, spiritual level, or whether we are attracted by a person just sexually, but find that person's thinking, character, interests and activities not very interesting.

Are we really concerned with that person's well-being and give him/her enough space and freedom to grow? Or are we just interested in that person for our own benefits?

The answers to such questions can come very early in a relationship, if we are honest enough to ask them ourselves. **Let your heart decide heart matters. Listen and feel within and you will know.** Your mind might say something totally different and spits out so many reasons speaking against a relationship.

I know that if both my wife and I would have listened only to our mind, we would not be together now.

Some people, men and women, are not yet ready for a really deep relationship with just one person, and prefer, even without being aware of this fact consciously, to have many relationships. One after the other or even at the same time. Do we desire monogamy or polygamy?

To enter a marriage and find out later that we choose polygamy, causes a lot of suffering and is certainly not the way to a happy lifestyle, especially when children are already present.

In the same way as we learned to attract happiness, health and wealth into our life, we can also attract our soul mate. The process works just as well, although you may need some patience. Because here we are dealing with a person who has his/her own desires and timetable.

It is not as easy as attracting the energies manifesting themselves as money. We deal with a personality and not an object. Our soul mate has free will and we need to trust that at the right time and circumstances we will meet.

This trust and patience, together with the strong desire to meet, is essential. And it will work!

When I was in my early twenties I suddenly got really fed up with all the more or less pleasant experiences with ladies. All the flirting and playing, the temporary successes and disappointments – it felt so shallow and superficial. I just wanted the real thing, to find the one and only special person.

So I decided to wait and apply what I knew to be true. As described above, I took my own "medicine".

For five years, I had no contact with women, except for shaking hands, or the occasional kiss on the cheek. And as my energies became stronger, so did my intense desire to meet Mrs. Right. My patience was tested and yet, my confidence that I will succeed was stronger. So, when we finally met, it was so obvious to both of us that "this is it!"

To meet your soul mate doesn't mean that we can now just relax and take it easy. Over the years my wife and I still had to work out some differences and make adjustments in the external world like finding a mutually satisfying and happy lifestyle. That is still necessary. And all I want to add here is that is was worth the efforts and the wait!

Natural stuff

So our desire to love and be loved is so natural. It is what gives us real satisfaction and real pleasure. On the ultimate level of our being, we are spirit. We are part of this higher principle which creates all the worlds on all their different energy levels.

Spirit energy creates and controls the mind. The mind creates our bodies, the physical world, and universe through the ethereal force.

We are all the children of the 'Great Spirit', without exceptions. On this level we are all equal and have the same amount of strength and creative energies at our disposal. This level is characterized by pure love and total happiness. Spirit is the celestial light which disperses all the clouds, all shadows, darkness and negativity.

The physical world that we live in now, is split into the two polarities. We perceive a split world where there is good and bad, health and sickness, up and down, rich and poor, cold and hot, male and female.

The Chinese describe the Tao as the holistic principle

which is divided into these *two poles of Yin and Yang*. Within each pole there is the seed for the opposite pole. The whole is intertwined and moves with its own dynamics.

Transcending this polarity is possible when we realize the spiritual energies of our deeper self. That's when we reach at least the position of neutrality. When we are aware of our spiritual nature and its basic qualities, we can't perceive others to be enemies. This concept exists only in the bipolar worlds defined by space and time.

From a spiritual point of view, we can see very clearly that we are all equal. *All people are spiritual people.* Nobody is more or less spiritual than somebody else! Spirit is spirit and once we understand the qualities of spirit, we also understand this.

What does make a difference, is the individual's *awareness* of his/her spirituality.

Some people may be more aware of it than others, but everybody could be fully aware of it.

Anyone, who chooses to be aware of his/her spiritual nature – anyone who truly wants to remember this deepest aspect of self – will easily know and experience it all! So there is, again, no need to struggle to become "enlightened" or whatever you want to call it. *It is a personal choice. To remember or not. Partially or fully. It is that easy!*

Club members

Now you may ask what does spiritual energy have to do with religion, or vice versa. Can we be spiritually aware without being religious, or, are religious persons spiritually aware?

The answers to these questions depend again on our definition of the words and also our perspective. Let's check it out.

Throughout history mankind has asked questions about our nature, about our origin and destination, and what life is all about anyway. Different religions and philosophies have originated in different parts of the world and at different times. Religion should be the attempt to answer these most basic questions we all ask ourselves sooner or later, depending on our age and situation in life. So religion is like the science of our spirituality and the universal laws affecting all of us, regardless of our race or culture. But is that really so?

Many people have become very skeptical about the role organized religions have played in our societies throughout history. And reject anything which sounds even remotely like religion. This is quite understandable to anyone who has studied a bit of world history.

Organized religions have always played an important role in the human development and we can see both positive and negative aspects and influences there. As with everything we choose to look at.

A thorough understanding of our spiritual nature will bring about peace and harmony. Because spirit is pure love. When we have no enemies, and we love instead of hate, then there are no more wars. Unfortunately, religious organizations have always played a major role in power politics. They meddled in the worldly affairs of the states and took their share of the bounty.

In my view, organized religion of any kind has failed to give us a deep spiritual understanding, as numerous, ongoing armed conflicts prove. And the last one hundred years have been particularly bloody. How come? Is there no spiritual truth to be found with these organizations? Where is the problem?

You probably noticed that I mentioned 'organized' religion and you may wonder why.

In a way, organized forms of religion are contradictions in themselves as they promote by their very nature disharmony and conflict instead of peace, harmony and happiness. How so?

Before any particular belief system can be incorporated and an organization formed, it must become a separate entity. The organizers have to first claim that they are the only ones to really know the absolute truth that sets us free. Right?

Let's say you want to start a new organization but you tell your audience that group A, B, C, and D, are in your opinion, preaching the correct and complete truth. How many people will agree to join your new group?

Nobody. If everybody can join group A, B, C, or D then there is no need for your group to exist!

So your first step will have to be to tell your listeners that group A, B, C and D have it all wrong, that they don't know the real truth or at best, are only partially correct. You must say that you have found the solution to All There Is. And if you are convincing enough you will succeed.

Companies work in the same way. You can not start a successful company and make a lot of money by telling your potential customers that the products of company A, B, C and D are just as good as yours. At the very least you have to tell them that your product is much cheaper while offering the same quality and benefits. Comparative advertising is not allowed in most countries although you may do it in the USA. So Company A can directly say something negative about its toughest competitor before staking their claims to superiority.

If you look at the world today we have not only the major recognized or historical denominations of religions looking to steadily expand their membership numbers, but within each denomination we find thousands of smaller groups. Never mind their names and sizes.

What they have in common is that they look for more people to join their particular faith and convictions.

The more members one group has, the more influence, power, money and respect they can yield. Members usually feel good to belong to a big, winning team. It increases self-esteem and the conviction that their group has it all right!

The more people share one belief the more they must be right. And of course group A with 100 million members and a war chest of billions of dollars is more likely to get a country's President's attention than group B with a hundred members only. In this sense, it is a survival of the fittest.

The increasing number of religious organizations engage in a kind of "warfare" and we can learn from history's lessons that this is not beneficial for peace at all. Of course, not all are holy crusaders in the traditional sense. Not all pick up arms. Most preaching nowadays is done with words, boycotts and political influence wrangling.

But an increasing amount of groups pick up weapons, trying to win converts to their way of life and belief system – or just wanting to get rid of the "unfaithful." It is a lot easier to disrupt our complex and globally-integrated civilization as new technologies are more vulnerable to disruptions and 'holy' terrorists can easily obtain relatively cheap, powerful weapons.

Just look at the subway sarin gas attacks recently in Tokyo as an example. In 1995 a Japanese cult with a worldwide following killed a dozen people and injured about 5000 others. For them, these attacks were just a test, much worse was planned. This group is still active even though their doomsday "guru" now sits in jail. Top notch scientists and academics became "club members" – they had a war chest with billions of dollars. And of course, they, too, thought that they have it all figured out and know it best.

All aspects of modern life, from financial systems, electricity distribution, water supply, car and air traffic systems, and so on, are controlled by computer systems. Some of these systems are still vulnerable to electronic attacks by hackers and all kinds of dissidents.

Another shortcoming of organized religion is their hierarchical systems. There are leaders of various levels, each commanding and expecting a certain degree of loyalty.

Members are supposed to follow their instructions. And there are plenty of examples of fighting for supremacy within a particular group. It looks very much like in politics, doesn't it?

Often leaders claim to be the only representative of God on earth and their words are supposed to be infallible. But they are men and women and are elected by other members of the group, are the founders of a group or just won their particular fight for leadership in other, perhaps unholy ways. Now members are expected to stop thinking independently and follow them blindly.

How can there be peace and harmony, brotherly and sisterly love and general happiness among mankind if we have so many organizations with 'infallible' leaders, all supposedly being "The" representative of God?

If God wanted to have one person representing Him/Her/It on Planet Earth, don't you think it would have been possible to declare with a voice from heaven that the one and only representative of God is always the person who is born with a purple skin?

We have brown, white, black and yellow races and it would certainly not be difficult for the Big Boss to make one person appear on planet Earth with purple skin! ***We should not expect that any form of organized religion can help mankind solve its problems because it has not worked in the past, does not work at present, and will most probably not work in the future, simply because the very nature of their existing is divisive rather than uniting.***

Of course there have been positive influences of religious organizations, too. As with everything, it is not just black or white. Charitable acts are inspired and organized by religious groups. Millions of people all over the world were taught to read and write. After all, that is a necessity before the individual study of holy scriptures becomes possible. Messages of hope have consoled people in grief and guided them through times of trouble.

And yes, thanks to all the experiences, both positive and negative, mankind has progressed to a level not known before in the recorded history. We have learned some things already from our mistakes.

But right now there is again a trend for further ethnic and religious fragmentation and fanatism. There are more and more divisions showing up and each new group is more determined to get it their way than ever before.

With the break up of the Soviet Union, the approaching new millennia, the spread of the information revolution, etc., more and more people are living in a particular ethnic area where a particular faith is generally practiced. And they look for reaffirmation. They want a strong sense of security, a sense of belonging, and they believe that they can get it that way.

We have four different stages of economic and mental development coexisting more or less peacefully at present.

In some parts of the world people still live in hunting and gathering societies with minimal contact to the modern world. Elsewhere, agriculture is the dominant economic way of life.

Those two forms of societies are generally operating in the mind set of tribalism.

Other countries are predominantly industrial age societies, where a larger cooperation among members of society is required. There is already a higher level of specialization needed for the perfect functioning and so nationalism is still the predominant thinking.

And elsewhere, we are seeing an increasing emerging of the information age, where the successful mind set is 'internationalism'.

Of course these four 'development' stages are intertwined and coexist in most countries, with some exceptions. Different countries are at different levels of modernization and most of them have the characteristics of the latter three stages to various degrees or percentages.

The globalization of the world has increased in the last decade especially thanks to the advancements in technology. So there is fewer and fewer places to hide from this new wave and general trend.

Some people feel threatened in their traditional way of life, they may feel insecure with all these changes going on and worry about their economic success and future. And the ethnic identity of their forefathers (respectively, mothers) is being challenged on a daily basis. This all adds to the confusion and brings about real identity crises.

Now some people choose to retreat in their little corner of known and fixed beliefs and decide to defend them stubbornly, at any price. Extremism and fundamentalism brought about by all these divisions in ethnic groupings, different cultures, economic and religious systems, are a real danger. All these smaller and bigger groups want to fight for supremacy, or at least their survival.

A new dawn

What is the solution to all this?

Obviously, we don't need and we don't want any more holy or economic wars. That would be a very sad mistake and a tragedy, especially since it is so unnecessary.

Once more and more of the leaders of the world's religions come to understand the role their organizations play in the division of the people, and they **recognize and respect the validity of all other belief systems**, then there is real hope. Of course, this understanding has to filter down all the ranks to the grass-roots level.

And it has to be followed up by concrete action or sometimes non-action, renouncing certain current activities, such as actively trying to find and convert people. If somebody went to a religious group and is interested to know about their ways and beliefs – that is voluntary, by choice, and therefore OK. But, how many groups and their members deliberately use fear as a tool to convert people – to so-called "save" them? Such fear-mongers divide the world in "us" and "them", the already "saved" and the poor souls that "need" to be saved. We have already looked into the reasons why some people look "down" on others and know that that's always a mistake.

Spiritual wisdom can be found in all denominations for people with open eyes, minds and hearts. Finding the really

important messages which unite us all are not hard to find for a spiritually-aware person. And yes, such people exist in all religious organizations all over the world. These people are working hard to bridge the gaps in the different understanding or interpretations. Hopefully, more and more people come to these conclusions, too.

Most people in the world have been born in a particular country, or part of a country, with a particular culture, where usually one or the other religion is predominant. Relatively few people make an active and individual choice, but rather follow the beliefs of their family. And a big part of this majority is not actively involved in their religion, but practice some rituals at special times only, such as births, weddings and funerals. Others are not interested at all and ignore religion altogether. But everybody has a certain level of spiritual awareness in common. Some more and some less.

These days, people travel to other parts of the world, live in a different culture, or marry a person from another country, culture or religion.

And more and more people are realizing that we are not that much different from each other. Despite the external differences of culture, race or religion. We humans all share common dreams and have similar basic desires. *International understanding, solidarity and cooperation is something very natural for our innermost self.*

Spirit doesn't make any distinction between such external factors as race or religious belief systems.

On this level there is no judgment of the "good, the bad and the ugly". A spiritually-aware person can still follow local traditions and customs, be proud of their country and so on.

But it is not possible to have an advanced spiritual understanding and at the same time have a "club mentality."

Thinking, that we are superior or better in any way because we live here or there, have this or that culture, economy, race or religion. This is simply not possible because it is against the very nature of spirit! It is totally contradicting and proves the lack of understanding of its very basic characteristics.

Many people all over the world have come to this understanding and they want to learn more about all of their aspects, including their innermost selves.

This new age awareness of all these people gives real hope for lasting peace, love and understanding everywhere. ***Welcome to the age of fun, the age of happiness!***

It is not at all necessary to practice any particular style of religion in order to become more aware of our own spirituality. Many people are very highly conscious and yet they don't belong to any specific organization. Yet, they recognize wisdom wherever they find it.

It is also not necessary to renounce one's lifelong religion and its practice to advance one's spiritual knowledge further. But what is a definite requirement is to give up any kind of club mentality. It is that simple!

It is important to see how things are in this world since we live here. When we get the bigger picture of why this and that happens, we don't need to become aggravated anymore. And who doesn't, when seeing particularly gruesome pictures about sectarian violence on TV, or when reading about the numerous atrocities still being committed.

Always remember your choice is to be happy. And we also decided to accept the world as it is.

So we don't need to be become depressed, as this would help nobody at all. And yet, we can't just close our eyes either. But sometimes we have to in order to experience love. It is easier with both eyes closed.

Sometimes it is hard to believe in love when we see hatred, war and violence. It is sometimes hard to believe in justice when seeing injustice in various forms. It is sometimes hard to feel wealthy and feel all the abundance when we struggle or witness people living in poverty.

And yet, when we close our eyes and travel within

towards our eternal and innermost being, we will perceive reality as it is, as it always was, and will be.

So, knowing that embarking on the road to our own happiness will also benefit the world and help to increase the happiness of all people, is certainly a comforting and happy thought. And that's how it really is! Let's see how it works.

A pleasant journey

Gaining a thorough understanding of our own spiritual nature will help us to reach another dimension of happiness.
And it is so easy, when we decide to be our own authority, go on the journey inwards and have trust in our experiences, and the goodness of it all.
All we really need to do is to listen within and make the conscious choice to want to remember it all again! With these easy steps all the doors are open, all the wisdom and joy can be picked up readily, increasingly, and without any limits!

Feeling our connection to the endless ocean of spirit is healing to all aspects of our self, including mind and body. It is invigorating, joyful and enlightening.

It is our birthright, as we are all a part of this energy. Whether we choose to give this energy a name or not has really no meaning or significance. Some may call it God, Father, or Mother. To many, the word "god" is too often used and abused, and negative associations come up. The same is true with other descriptions or names like Allah, Buddha, Jehovah, etc. This is entirely understandable. So, any name or no name is fine. It works just as well.

But, let's call it 'Great Spirit' for the remainder of this book, so we know what we're talking about. Just substitute it with something of your choice, if you prefer to do so. From now on, I don't use capital letters for 'great spirit' – to emphasize that this is just another description of something which is difficult to describe.

Some people say absolutely that this is all hogwash and that there is no absolute truth. But isn't such an absolute statement a contradiction to their opinion that there are no absolutes?

As said before, this is a world to be *experienced.* It has nothing to do with beliefs or not. It is what we experience as an individual. If you have no such experiences, then for you it is not true. And if you have made some experiences, then you know that it is true.

It is not a blind belief, but your personal knowledge of a personal experience.

There is no point to argue about such things as we all make our individual experiences. And some may not. Or they don't remember them, at this moment.

Imagine the great spirit to be the sun and each one of us is a sun ray. This sun ray is of the same quality as the sun, without any differences. But obviously one sun ray has less quantity or "weight" than the whole sun.

The sun ray originates from the big pool of spirit, the sun, and travels throughout the universe. It travels all over and visits all kinds of planets and stars.

Once reaching a particular planet like planet Earth, the sun ray adjusts itself to the energy vibrations of this dimension by creating itself the necessary vehicle to explore it. It creates itself a mind and through the ethereal force, a body. Now it is free to check it all out, everything this planet has to offer.

The body gets sustained by the energies available at the proper vibration level of this planet. And the sun ray gets more and more involved in the everyday experiences. So much so, that it suddenly forgets about where it came from and what it is all about.

When playing with other children you don't want to be constantly reminded that you are not really the hero you pretend to be. After some time, all the playing becomes boring and the sunray starts to wonder what else there is. At some point it leaves. Maybe back home or maybe some-place else.

Maybe the earthly body's energies are used up because

the sun ray forgot about nourishing it properly, or it was due to an accident while playing, or maybe it was just time to go.

The sun ray is always connected to the sun. But with all the playing and fooling around, the illusions of the great game have covered the sun with clouds, blocking it from sight.

Once the sun ray was curious and looked up. And it suddenly noticed that there is a connection leading upwards. It concentrated for a while and the clouds started to disappear. All of a sudden it saw the sun and knew that this is where it came from. That it is a part of the sun, too.

This realization made the sun ray very happy and it continued to play. But every day it took the time to look up, enjoying the warmth and strength of the sun. And continued to live happily ever after, knowing that there is always a home to return to.

The key to making this wonderful experience is that you ***really want to*** make it, that you want to remember the deepest aspect of your self. Then, you will.

The easiest way to an ever more fulfilling spiritual experience is through the aspect of love. This is the central characteristics of spiritual energy.

In our meditation we can feel the spirit energy of our self and we can connect to the ocean of the great spirit simply by stating:

"I want to feel the great spirit's love for me!" Or, if you prefer it a bit more prayer like: "Please let me feel your unconditional love for me!"

Then all you need to do is to feel within and experience this love. It will accept you the way you are, without any conditions. It will embrace you, hug you and cherish you. And you will feel stronger and happier. Try it out, it works!

The great spirit's love for all its parts, or children if you like, is always there and it is ***completely equal.***

For the "good, bad and the ugly." It doesn't make such distinctions and therefore no conditions are imposed on this love. Real love is never partial, otherwise it would not be perfect! It just is. Always.

Imagine again the mother, who loves both of her children with pure love. And that means the one who sometimes behaves naughty and the one that is always sweet. Nevertheless, she loves them both equally and doesn't wish either of them any harm. But knowing, that they have their own life to live, she gives them both free will to make their own choices in life.

We all have been given this basic freedom. **The freedom to choose. It is an integral part of any person, of every spirit.** So whatever we do while we live and play here, is our responsibility.

The energies of our creative and destructive processes in life will somehow or another become balanced again. This is how the overall balance is maintained. That's how it works.

Some people choose more or less consciously to direct their anger and blame towards the great spirit because they feel neglected, somehow suffer or simply because their prayers were not answered. And finally they may come to the point where they reject themselves, their own goodness, their own heritage.

Suffering is never ordered or prescribed by the great spirit because it is pure love. And such love is understanding and not judging or condemning. When we suffer, we brought it entirely to ourselves by attracting it into our life. Somehow or another.

There is really no one else to blame, even if we want to. This may be hard to realize but nevertheless that's how it is.

Ultimately, the suffering brought about by fears, especially the fear of death, and overcoming the grief of losing loved ones, is only possible when we realize our eternal essence as pure spirit.

Some may reject their spiritual origin and nature because they don't like the idea that there is something greater than they are. And they think of themselves in terms of their bodies and mind only, maybe a particularly smart, beautiful and powerful one, though.

They prefer to play master here and the traditional picture of a "lord of the universe", who controls everything and everybody, is simply in the way of that desire.

But that again is *not* how it is. If they knew about their own heritage with its unlimited greatness and power, they could not feel that way.

And since we have free will, we are not controlled by the great spirit. We can do whatever we want, make even the most serious of mistakes. ***And we are not judged but ultimately we judge ourselves, and decide freely to work things out again!***

Somehow or another we restore the balance. We all are the masters of our own destiny. And ultimately, this is so without any time limits.

Once the sun ray again basked in the sunlight and clearly saw where it came from. And it also noticed that there are billions and billions of other sun rays. It realized, that all the people here on planet Earth have come from just the same place and are identical in quality and size. They are not bigger or smaller, they are not richer or poorer. They are not black and white, smart or dumb. No, they are equal.

"Wow!" it thought, "This is really great! I will probably have to adjust my behavior here a little bit. I can feel such a deep love for my neighbor and yet I shouted at him just yesterday! Oh, well, I will make it up and I will show him somehow that I love and care."

Now it is quite obvious that a person who knows of his/her ultimately spiritual nature, and has experienced the inherent qualities of spirit, will be automatically kind to all sisters and brothers. ***Being kind is not a sign of weakness but strength. Real strength.***

When you treat others with real kindness, you will make it very hard for them to treat you badly – cheat you, trick you and the like.

Kids often don't learn kindness at home. But instead, learn to become tough and unkind to others in order to get what they want, trying constantly to outsmart, exploit others, respond in kind and all that. Small wonder if a person has never experienced kindness firsthand.

It is not a happy way of going through life, even while driving the latest model vehicle.

Be strong, but always try to respond in kindness. The real kind. ***It will work wonders in even unlikely situations...***

To experience the pure love of spirit is a real eye opener. This love is understanding, unconditional and impartial. And finally we can pass on this love to all the people we live with or meet. And we can send it wherever we want to.

It is simply not possible to experience such a love and then go out into the world to rob and steal, maim and kill.

Such acts are only possible without having made any true progress on the way to our innermost self.

So some people truly think that all they really are, is a piece of flesh, blood and bones, controlled by a superior brain and that after maybe seventy years they will cease to exist completely.

Are such people more or less inclined to behave in a predatory way than a person who has experienced his/her spirituality? And are they more or less inclined to have racist views than someone who knows that we are all brothers and sisters?

Fortunately, many people are still undecided one way or the other and they choose to behave morally, just in case. They know that following the laws and common-sense ethics is the smart way to go for a trouble-free life and the functioning of a peaceful and prosperous society.

Some people are afraid to behave bad in any way because they are god-fearing people. And others follow the rules of their particular religion so blindly that they have totally given up their independent thinking. Such people can be turned by unscrupulous leaders into armed and dangerous zealots, ready to destroy anybody fed to them as being an 'enemy of god'. They perceive their fellow human beings as enemies just because they don't follow their religion with its particular dogmas. Such people don't really understand the true message and meaning of their own religion yet.

Religions teach love – none of the major religions preach hate. How can a person claim to be a true member of A, B, C or D and then go out and throw a bomb somewhere?

Following dogmas and rituals, in my experience, have no practical meaning to the understanding of spirit. They are usually symbolic, rooted in history and meant to distinguish one group from another. Or they bind its members more closely together. Dogmas and rituals are often needed to keep up a particular hierarchical structure. Among new age followers and practitioners we can find some that, although they may reject old dogmas, invent new ones and think that they are more valid because they are different....

All hate is the absence of love. All darkness is the absence of light. Wherever true love is present, the celestial light immediately brightens up everything and everybody.

As we become happier and happier, enjoying ourselves and feeling full of this celestial light and love, it will increase the vibration level of all the energies. And ultimately of the whole world and everybody in it.

Have you ever gone to a supermarket when you felt really happy and good? And noticed that the cashier often looks quite unhappy? Did you see how she returned your smile when she saw you smiling broadly, being friendly to her and in a good mood?

Smiles and a happy mood can be so contagious! Once a cashier told me how good she felt because I was the first person that day who smiled and cheerfully talked to her, and that she had given up smiling to people on the job because they are often unfriendly and treat her like a maid or worse!

We already know that we can not change the world easily by ourselves. We can do our best to contribute in various ways here and there. But simply to become a truly happy person will make a lot of difference.

Even if not much change to the better happens while we are here, at least we have a good time, enjoy ourselves at best and are happy!

And suddenly, as more and more people decide to put their first priority into increasing their personal happiness, everybody becomes happy! What a happy thought!

One day, we as a society will maybe decide to look up to, admire and follow the footsteps of the happy people of the world. Rather than just glorifying power, money and fame, or fighting about silly notions, such as, who is right and who is wrong.

It doesn't really matter to the happy people because they are busy being happy. And they don't care for the admiration of others. There is no need or desire to stand in the limelight or develop the disease of "guru-itis."

And lift- off

Can it get any better?

You bet it can. And it will. So brace yourself for the final lift-off. Although we connected ourselves to the ultimate love of our self and the great spirit, we can still go a step further.

Once we feel that love, we can return and send it back to the sun, the great spirit.

Even without knowing exactly what it is. It doesn't matter because one day we will find out and just know! In the meantime, let's simply experience and enjoy this loving energy.

To *actively* return this love is again more pleasurable and fulfilling than just being loved by it.

Give it a try and you will experience it for yourself! ***Once you have experienced this active mode of loving, you can send this spiritual love to your parents, brothers and sisters, your soul mate, to anybody you feel like.***

And hey, remember to love yourself in this same way, too! Not just as being Black or White, American or French, general manager or cashier, Catholic or Jew. But as an eternal, bright and strong, lovable and loving, joyful and happy part of the great spirit.

This is the ultimate gift you can make to yourself, and to everybody else. It is a quiet way of giving and you can not expect anything in return. But it will again increase your happiness.

And when the love you feel in your heart is overflowing and you don't know where to send it to anymore, you may always send it to a politician or a person rotting away in jail for mistakes committed, or the hungry, needy and poor people of the world. It is up to you!

This loving spiritual energy is the most powerful there is, and it is soothing and healing, comforting and strengthening. After all, we are all made out of the same 'material'. On this spiritual level we are all friends, brothers and sisters. And we might as well relate to each other that way!

We already looked at what happens if we send angry and condemning vibes to say, a politician. What happens to us and our happiness when we connect and exchange energy of lower frequencies. That person is less likely to be able to do much good or make the right decisions after receiving such vibes.

It is degrading, rather than uplifting. If you expect a person to be a bad person and do bad things, is that person more or less likely to behave that way than if you don't?

Whenever we send pure love, it will have only beneficial effects on that person. Chances are much better that beneficial decisions will be made, benefiting all of us.

Real love is not intrusive or manipulative ever. When you want a plant to grow up faster, it would be definitely wrong to just pull it from the top. It would become uprooted and die. The only way to go is to give the plant the proper amount of water, nutrients and light.

Nobody can help another person by sharing some suffering. But we can help by being strong and sharing this unlimited strength.

Sending out real love is strengthening a person in a gentle way, the part of the person we all are in essence. When the sun ray becomes stronger, it will more easily remember the sun and bask in the celestial light: the light and love of home.

Living in this love and loving this love will dispel all the clouds floating in the way to our complete and never ending happiness. And it will be like the sun ray living now closer to its home, where the intense light of the sun prevents all future clouds from ever forming again.

You know that *you* are the solution. And you know how it's done. **Make yourself happy.** And stay that way! If that's what you want.

Experience the spiritual love of the great spirit and know that it is always there for you whenever you want it.

Know and experience that this spiritual energy has unlimited power and can express itself in unlimited ways.

It can be happiness, health, wealth, strength, wisdom. You name it and you can get it! Make it express itself into your life, in every dimension, and all the time!

The great spirit only 'wills' the best for all because it is all love. And remember, that it is our choice whether we can accept it or not!

Once you fully understand this as a fact you are holding the ultimate key to a very happy life.

This knowledge fully integrates all the previously discussed realizations and propels it to ever new heights. It is the total integration of our mind, willpower, creativity and spiritual awareness with the great spirit's well wishing, power and love.

When you know that the great spirit wants, or rather, wishes you to be happy, healthy and strong, wealthy and wise.

That is the supreme wish.

And since we are a part of the great spirit, **all we need to do now is to agree** with this wish. And say: "I fully agree, that's what I want, too!"

Feel this reality, know this reality, and yes, experience this reality, every day and all the time!

I hope that now you can truly say: "Yes I am happy now!" One day we might bump into each other on the street somewhere, somehow. And we might laugh at each other and decide to throw a party! A party to celebrate life and be happy!

So long, my friend!

PS: You are very welcome to visit me in cyberspace, give your feedback and communicate with me and fellow readers at: http://www.beampublishing.com

REALIZATION 85~99

•

I am spirit, mind and body!

•

The highest energy is spirit!

•

My eternal essence is spirit!

•

Spirit is pure love!

•

Love is always!

•

Pure love is unconditional and impartial!

•

The great spirit loves me!

•

I want to feel this love!

•

I want to return this love!

•

I love the great spirit and all!

•

- *I want to remember it all!*

- *I do remember, always!*

- *The great spirit wishes me to be happy, healthy, wealthy and wise!*

- *I agree to be happy, healthy, wealthy and wise!*

- *Yes I am happy now!*

-

Appendix:

All Realizations

Here again are all the realizations we have made together. Sometimes, when you feel less happy than you wish to be, open these pages at random. Concentrate first on your desire to be happy and then point your finger somewhere along these lines, wishing to know the answer to your problem.

Then open your eyes and read the realization shown. Remember it fully, the reasons why you came to this realization and agree with it once more! Often when reading it again, your complete memory will come back instantly.

It will help you along your way out of a temporary problem and towards renewed happiness!

You will find next to each realization some space where you can tick either: "I agree", "I'm not sure yet", or "I don't agree." Use differently colored pens each time you go through. Start with a red or green pen, a few months later, go through it again with a blue one, etc. Put a date at the beginning in the particular color of the pen used each time.

It may be hard to agree to some realizations at first. You may agree somewhat, but not fully. At times you may not be sure one way or the other.

Whatever you have experienced firsthand, you will understand and agree easily.

Read again the text leading to a realization that you don't agree with and reflect on this issue deeply from within. When you meditate, ask yourself if this is true or not.

And if you don't agree with a particular realization, ask yourself why you don't. Sometimes, when an issue is really affecting us, a part of us refuses to understand and realize what we really should come to realize.

The harder your opposition to an issue is, the more you have a reason to work it out. Such issues then tend to show up in your life, until they are resolved.

So take up this list from time to time and go especially through the realizations you can't agree with.

Often you will find that a few months later, you will suddenly agree with it.

No opposition anymore. And it happened without much effort either!

So here we go:

		I agree	I'm not sure yet	I don't agree
1:	I choose to be happy!	☐	☐	☐
2:	My happiness is my first priority!	☐	☐	☐
3:	I want to be happy, healthy, and wealthy!	☐	☐	☐
4:	I decide to be happy now!	☐	☐	☐
5:	I have no excuse for not being happy now!	☐	☐	☐
6:	I can enjoy every moment of my life!	☐	☐	☐
7:	I am mindful all the time!	☐	☐	☐
8:	I don't mind changes!	☐	☐	☐
9:	I am very flexible!	☐	☐	☐
10:	I love to laugh and smile!	☐	☐	☐
11:	I can see funny things all the time!	☐	☐	☐
12:	I listen to my feelings within!	☐	☐	☐
13:	I trust and follow my feelings!	☐	☐	☐
14:	I know what I want to experience and enjoy!	☐	☐	☐
15:	I can always see something positive!	☐	☐	☐
16:	I am careful and enjoy myself all the time!	☐	☐	☐
17:	All my dreams can become true!	☐	☐	☐
18:	Everything is energy rotating at different vibrations!	☐	☐	☐
19:	Every cause produces an effect, every effect has a cause!	☐	☐	☐

	I agree	I'm not sure yet	I don't agree
20: Energy changes its form, but continues to exist!	☐	☐	☐
21: What is within, is without. The external reflects the internal!	☐	☐	☐
22: All energy flows create an energy field!	☐	☐	☐
23: Everything is connected with each other!	☐	☐	☐
24: Energy of similar wave length resonate together!	☐	☐	☐
25: Similar energies attract each other!	☐	☐	☐
26: I am multi-dimensional!	☐	☐	☐
27: I desire harmony in everything!	☐	☐	☐
28: I can meditate to relax and expand myself!	☐	☐	☐
29: I always express myself positively!	☐	☐	☐
30: I express myself clearly and precisely!	☐	☐	☐
31: I concentrate on positive thoughts!	☐	☐	☐
32: I speak only positively about people!	☐	☐	☐
33: I always communicate the truth!	☐	☐	☐
34: My word is good as gold!	☐	☐	☐
35: I accept myself as I am!	☐	☐	☐
36: I respect myself the way I am!	☐	☐	☐
37: I love myself as I am!	☐	☐	☐
38: I can not be exploited!	☐	☐	☐
39: I don't need to exploit others!	☐	☐	☐
40: I help others and accept their help!	☐	☐	☐
41: I attract all the people into my life!	☐	☐	☐
42: I enjoy the company of happy people!	☐	☐	☐
43: I respect all opinions!	☐	☐	☐
44: I don't need to have too many opinions!	☐	☐	☐
45: I can change my opinions!	☐	☐	☐
46: I can be quiet!	☐	☐	☐

	I agree	I'm not sure yet	I don't agree
47: I don't need to compete!	☐	☐	☐
48: I don't like to argue!	☐	☐	☐
49: I can not be intimidated!	☐	☐	☐
50: I don't need to intimidate others!	☐	☐	☐
51: I don't want to be angry anymore!	☐	☐	☐
52: I don't need to become angry!	☐	☐	☐
53: I don't need to limit my preferences!	☐	☐	☐
54: I am mainly attached to my happiness!	☐	☐	☐
55: I have less expectations!	☐	☐	☐
56: I am patient!	☐	☐	☐
57: I respect the free will of all!	☐	☐	☐
58: I don't need to control others!	☐	☐	☐
59: I accept the world as it is!	☐	☐	☐
60: I know and understand what caused my anger!	☐	☐	☐
61: I decide to release all past anger!	☐	☐	☐
62: We all make mistakes!	☐	☐	☐
63: I know when I made a mistake!	☐	☐	☐
64: I can admit my mistakes!	☐	☐	☐
65: I understand and learn from my mistakes!	☐	☐	☐
66: I am tolerant of mistakes mine and others!	☐	☐	☐
67: I do not need to feel guilty!	☐	☐	☐
68: I don't want to blame or judge!	☐	☐	☐
69: I accept all people the way they are!	☐	☐	☐
70: I see people as they are now!	☐	☐	☐
71: I don't want to be afraid!	☐	☐	☐
72: I do not need to be afraid!	☐	☐	☐
73: I don't need to be sick!	☐	☐	☐
74: I don't need to suffer to learn!	☐	☐	☐
75: I forgive because I understand and forget!	☐	☐	☐

	I agree	I'm not sure yet	I don't agree
76: I deserve to be happy, healthy and wealthy!	☐	☐	☐
77: I am motivated by signs of success!	☐	☐	☐
78: I am content with all aspects of my life!	☐	☐	☐
79: Money is energy and available to me all in abundance!	☐	☐	☐
80: I feel rich and wealthy!	☐	☐	☐
81: All energy including money is free!	☐	☐	☐
82: I love and accept free money!	☐	☐	☐
83: I am rich!	☐	☐	☐
84: I get all that I want!	☐	☐	☐
85: I am spirit, mind and body!	☐	☐	☐
86: The highest energy is spirit!	☐	☐	☐
87: My eternal essence is spirit!	☐	☐	☐
88: Spirit is pure love!	☐	☐	☐
89: Love is always!	☐	☐	☐
90: Pure love is unconditional and impartial!	☐	☐	☐
91: The great spirit loves me!	☐	☐	☐
92: I want to feel this love!	☐	☐	☐
93: I want to return this love!	☐	☐	☐
94: I love the great spirit and all!	☐	☐	☐
95: I want to remember it all!	☐	☐	☐
96: I do remember, always!	☐	☐	☐
97: The great spirit wishes me to be happy, healthy, wealthy and wise!	☐	☐	☐
98: I agree to be happy, healthy, wealthy and wise!	☐	☐	☐
99: Yes I am happy now!	☐	☐	☐

Our Special Guarantee of Satisfaction

Yes I am Happy Now! is more than a book. It is a road map for a new, happier and more fulfilling way of life. For you, and for others. It is a road map we follow and believe in – that's why we wrote and published the book, to share this vision and this journey.

However, though we believe these truths are universal, we know that this book will not be for everyone. That is why we offer this remarkable guarantee:

If you are not satisfied that **Yes I am Happy Now!** delivers on its promise of showing you one path towards a life fulfilled with happiness and success, Arne will donate his royalties on this book to Scudo (Latin for "Protective Shield") – an organization run by a group of dedicated volunteers – that is actively protecting and re-foresting tropical rainforests in Australia – helping to make the world a better, happier place for all of us.

To exercise this guarantee, here's all you need to do:

1. Donate your copy of **Yes I am Happy Now!** to a public library, a prison library or a school library.

2. Send us a copy of the receipt they provide you to this address:

    Beam Publishing USA
    2875 S. Nellis Blvd., A8 – PMB 241
    Las Vegas, NV 89121

When you do that, we will make a donation in your name to Scudo. You will be helping others in two ways:

1. You'll be sharing **Yes I am Happy Now!** with others who might find in this book the value that was missing for you.

2. You will be helping to preserve and restore vital rainforests.

We hope that, even if this book doesn't make you happy, our unique guarantee will make you happy – so that, at least a moment, you can say, **"Yes I am Happy Now!"**

Arne Klingenberg
Author, Yes I am Happy Now!

Beam Publishing
http://www.beampublishing.com

P.S. You may find more information about Scudo on our website.

Notes:

www.ingramcontent.com/pod-product-compliance
Lightning Source LLC
Chambersburg PA
CBHW021102080526
44587CB00010B/339